Heritage Revitalisation for Tourism in Hong Kong

Heritage tourism is a global multi-million-dollar phenomenon, influencing national, regional and local cultural identities. Hong Kong finds itself at the confluence of several post-colonial economic, political and social developments and with this comes a greater awareness of the need for more meaningful cultural and heritage tourism products, especially in the form of revitalised heritage attractions.

Taking a qualitative approach and using semi-structured in-depth interviews with practitioners and stakeholders in the field, this study explores the role of interpretation in heritage revitalisation projects for tourism in Hong Kong. It seeks to examine why the interpretive element of these projects so often gets diminished during the course of implementation and outlines five propositions that may inform it going forward. Ultimately, the findings of this study suggest that, as issues of local identity become ever more important in Hong Kong, the role of interpretation in the development of its heritage tourism products needs to be holistic, integrated and consistent across public, private and non-governmental sectors.

Developing a framework of understanding to identify the contextual issues of interpretation and commodification, this book will be useful to students and scholars of tourism, heritage studies and Asian studies more generally.

Chris White is founder of Winkle-picker Ltd, a specialist interpretive planning consultancy for museums and heritage tourism. He has worked in the field of museum master planning and design for some of the most famous institutions worldwide for over 25 years. He holds a Doctorate in Hospitality and Tourism Management and is a Fellow of the Royal Society of Arts.

Routledge Focus on Asia

Heritage Revitalisation for Tourism in Hong Kong
The Role of Interpretive Planning

Chris White

Routledge
Taylor & Francis Group

LONDON AND NEW YORK

First published 2019
by Routledge

2 Park Square, Milton Park, Abingdon, Oxfordshire OX14 4RN
52 Vanderbilt Avenue, New York, NY 10017

Routledge is an imprint of the Taylor & Francis Group, an informa business

First issued in paperback 2019

British Library Cataloguing-in-Publication Data
A catalogue record for this book is available from the British Library

Library of Congress Cataloging-in-Publication Data
A catalog record has been requested for this book

ISBN: 978-1-138-61488-8 (hbk)
ISBN: 978-0-367-46513-1 (pbk)

Typeset in Times New Roman
by Wearset Ltd, Boldon, Tyne and Wear

For my family

Contents

Figures

Tables

Acknowledgements

I would like to thank Professor Bob McKercher of the Hong Kong Polytechnic University for his help, encouragement and guidance throughout the research and writing of the original study.

1 Introduction

In October 2014, in the London Borough of Tower Hamlets, planning permission was granted by the council for the change of use of a Victorian building to a new museum on the women of the East End and the suffragettes. It was intended to be a localised celebration of women's social history focused on one of the most vibrant and diverse areas of the capital. As stated by the planning document:

> The museum will recognise and celebrate the women of the East End who have shaped history, telling the story of how they have been instrumental in changing society. It will analyse the social, political and domestic experience from the Victorian period to the present day.

In August 2015, it opened as The Jack the Ripper Museum.

Admittedly an extreme example, this case demonstrates the need for a clear interpretive mission to be articulated at the beginning of a project and carried through to implementation in the process of developing a heritage attraction. In this instance, it was not just a matter of the storytelling being diminished in the end product but of it somehow being perverted from its original stated objective through a flawed interaction between the public and private heritage attraction sectors. A potentially meaningful local attraction that could have had a wider tourism appeal somehow became the crassest of tourism products. As Hong Kong enters a new era of heritage tourism with flagship revitalisation schemes forming a significant part of its promotional impetus, lessons from around the world (including relatively mature heritage attraction markets such as the UK) like these need to be learned and built into any heritage attraction development model going forward.

The tourism industry in 2017 contributed to just over 10% of the world's GDP and employed nearly 10% of its workforce. The global heritage tourism industry is a multi-million-dollar phenomenon which impacts on national, regional and local aspects of cultural identity. Cultural heritage attractions are subject to the same vagaries identified by tourism theory that apply to other types of destination such as host-destination models (Leiper, 1995; Mill and Morrison, 1985; Hall, 1995), motivation (Richards, 2002), distance decay (Beaman, 1974; Bull, 1991; McKercher, 1998a; McKercher and Lew, 2003), market access (McKercher, 1998b), tourist behaviour (Lew and McKercher, 2006; Moutinho, 2001), finite time budgets (McKean *et al.*, 1995), and destination lifecycles (Butler, 1980; Plog, 1974, 2001). However, working in the field of heritage and museum attraction development in the UK, Middle East, Singapore and Hong Kong, I have over 25 years witnessed the lack of connection between academic theories related to macro cultural/heritage tourism and the government/commercial practice of heritage revitalisation.

Obviously, in order to have a heritage tourism draw you need to have preserved some heritage in the first place. Post-war Hong Kong has been notoriously unsentimental about its built heritage. It is one of the world's ultimate urban landscapes and has a mature tourism market with well-established and recently completed heritage attractions; this despite a relative lack of heritage assets compared to other world cities. In the last 50 years, heritage conservation policy in Hong Kong has moved from a narrow focus on pre-Colonial archaeology to a broader, more inclusive approach that incorporates the wider public and geographic areas rather than individual buildings. There has been a growing appreciation of the value of cultural and heritage assets (as witnessed by the increased public activism since the removal of the Central Star Ferry in 2006) resulting in more built heritage assets being considered by the government as consumable heritage commodities for adaptive re-use as new venues of entertainment, education and the arts. The importance of built heritage conservation to both the identity of the people and city of Hong Kong, as well as the tourist industry, has been recognised. We can now see the maxim of "adapt or die" being applied in the revitalisation of heritage buildings for a variety of uses. However, this approach is a relatively recent phenomenon and it remains to be seen how successful the Hong Kong government will be in implementing it. There are already examples such as the Marine Police Headquarters in Tsim Sha Tsui completed in 2009 to reflect upon which experts in the field agree fell short of expectations in many ways; it is more often cited as an example of how not to adaptively re-use a heritage site that has served as a warning for subsequent projects. At the end of 2017, the Blue House cluster in Wanchai, providing residential and community services, won the Award of Excellence in the UNESCO Asia-Pacific Awards for Cultural Heritage Conservation. Whilst this is a small-scale project primarily aimed at the community, it shows that developments in this field are starting to go in the right direction.

Key to so many of these projects for government support is the need to tell the story of the site. This requires the insertion of interpretation or interpretive planning into the revitalisation process. However, there is, at a pivotal point of the development process of heritage attractions, something of a theoretical and practical void in terms of how the twin forces of interpretation and commodification actually work. And it is this fissure that we intend to explore.

This interpretation/commodification nexus sees the cultural/heritage interpretive practitioner frequently operating within the context of an architecturally and commercially-led project. Within a development team of competing agendas such as new build architecture or commercial real estate (the practitioners of which have ready tools for quantifying the value of their work to the project and society as a whole), interpretation can sometimes find itself "put on the back burner" as more quantifiable elements of the project take priority. This may be the case even when telling the story of the site is widely promoted as the *raison d'être* for spending large amounts of public money. As more adaptive re-use projects, which involve both public money and the alteration of public heritage assets, come on stream in Hong Kong and elsewhere in Asia this will be an increasingly important issue if storytelling is to remain at the heart of the impetus behind such projects.

This study aims to answer the following question:

> Why – when the stated primary intention of so many urban heritage revitalisation projects is to tell the story of the site for the purposes of cultural tourism – does the interpretive element of these projects so often get diminished during the course of implementation and what can be done about it?

The objectives of the study, therefore, are to:

- Develop a framework of understanding that allows us to focus on the theoretical and practical role of interpretation in heritage revitalisation projects for tourism
- Identify the contextual issues related to the position of interpretation within the development process of such projects
- Use qualitative research through interviews with key professionals and stakeholders to reveal perspectives on the role of interpretation in these projects
- Analyse these findings and formulate ways in which they might inform the role of interpretation in such projects going forward

Definition of terms

As a relatively obscure area of the heritage tourism and creative industries, it is important that the terms we use within the study are clearly understood:

Heritage tourism: Cultural or heritage tourism is both an established and growing driver of the world economy in the "developed" and "developing" worlds. In broad terms, cultural or heritage tourism is travel with a purpose of learning or experiencing another culture (Adams and Roy, 2007). It has been observed that all travel is some form of cultural tourism, that it is omnipresent and omnipotent (Richards, 2007; Smith, 2009). Whilst the academic study of heritage tourism, along with other forms of tourism, is a relatively recent phenomenon, the activity itself is clearly not and can be traced back to as early as 1500 BCE (Zueglow, 2016).

Heritage revitalisation: a relatively new concept that recognises the need for heritage properties to be able to financially sustain themselves through their operations. As a late-comer to heritage conservation, the Hong Kong SAR Government has embraced the idea of heritage revitalisation through "adaptive re-use" of heritage buildings as a means to open up historic buildings for public use whilst reducing the burden for the taxpayer of ongoing subsidy, as well as regenerating areas of the city and sectors of the economy. The Commissioner for Heritage's website states that "we are committed to put our historic buildings to good adaptive re-use. We aim to give these buildings a new lease of life for the enjoyment of the public". It is a field which encompasses conservation, tourism and urban planning with links to museology, real estate and arts management. Across all the tangible attractions, the most common vehicle for encouraging interaction with or learning about the site is some form of museum – whether that be purpose-built, integrated into existing architectural fabric or open-air.

Heritage attraction design: the need for attractions has seen it incorporated into the "5 As" of tourism (Attractions, Accommodation, Access, Activities and Amenities), commonly accepted as pre-requisites for a functioning tourist system. These have been classified into a hierarchy of primary (an initial draw to tourists from outside the region), secondary (a draw for tourists already in the region) and tertiary (of local interest) (Bull, 1991). A revitalised heritage attraction could potentially fit into any of these categories but given the investment required for conservation, restoration and adaptive re-use it is more likely that it would be regarded as a primary or secondary attraction. The link between heritage and heritage attraction design is the point at which the process begins to turn the heritage asset into a commodity. Of particular interest is the point at which interpretation and commodification interact in the development of a heritage tourism revitalisation project. A museum-like experience for the visitor might range from a very small museum consisting of graphic panels and some artefacts, to an immersive audio-visual experience, to an outdoor trail. Most visitor centres incorporate museum-like exhibition techniques and often act as an essential anchor to a range of offers, providing a convenient location for practical visitor facilities such as information desks, toilets, souvenir shops and staff offices.

Interpretive planning: this term is used throughout the study to refer to an initial step in the planning and design process for public educational attractions which may also have a tourism or entertainment purpose such as museums, science centres, zoos, heritage sites and other cultural facilities. It is a decision-making process that rationalises client requirements and resources with visitor needs and expectations to determine the most effective way to communicate key messages to target audiences through various display media, management provisions or educational programming. Interpretive is used an adjective to describe these activities.

Interpretation: this term is used to describe the product of the interpretive planning process or the ways in which information is communicated at heritage or cultural attractions.

Why is it important?

Cultural or heritage tourism has been a phenomenon worldwide from the earliest times. It could be said that curiosity about the next village is intrinsic to what it is to be human. This type of tourism has also been successfully commodified from ancient times, creating both a contemporary and historical network of infrastructure, custom and narratives. In more recent times, "the tourism industry and experiences enjoyed by tourists were both shaped by and helped to create the modern world ... tourism emerged as a central component of the 'modern world' and of the controversial notion of 'modernity'" (Zueglow, 2016).

As an activity, it is universally seen as a means of broadening the mind and cultivating manners, sophistication and the soul. It has had a two-way, widespread and profound cultural impact, changing landscapes and being shaped by prevailing social concerns, providing fixed assets of identity and, to use Hemingway's apt phrase, "moveable feasts" of experiences for countless millions.

As one of the fastest growing sectors in the world economy, it is an important creator of new jobs – around one in ten. Tourism is the main export for a third of developing countries and in some small island states can represent 25% of GDP. It is hard to estimate how much of this tourism is for the sole purpose of visiting a cultural or heritage site but estimates by the WTO puts the desire to experience heritage places as a motivating factor for around 40% of tourism trips.

Defining what constitutes a heritage tourist is difficult but the market is huge. The World Travel and Tourism Council (WTTC) estimated that in 2015 the UK travel and tourism industry as a whole directly generated a £68.6 billion gross value added contribution to UK GDP (3.7%). In the same year, domestic and international tourists made 192 million trips to visit the UK's cultural, historic and natural assets. Heritage tourism also supported an estimated £20.2 billion contribution to the UK GDP (over 1.1%) and 386,000 jobs. The heritage tourism sector itself generated an £8.8 billion gross contribution to the UK economy, exceeding other major cultural sectors such as the music, performing, and visual arts sectors combined. And what are visitors spending their money on? Domestic day tourists are more likely to visit natural heritage attractions, while domestic overnight and overseas visitors are slightly more likely to visit built heritage and museums/galleries (Oxford Economics, 2016). Visit Britain, which surveys demand and success rates for tourists to the UK, regards cultural/heritage tourism as the most important part of British tourism, touching as it does some aspect of every trip to the country.

Since the end of World War II, the worldwide demand for cultural or heritage tourism experiences has increased dramatically, whether that be for reasons of religious pilgrimage, visits to places of literary, industrial or (increasingly) cinematic/televisual significance, to trace family heritage, or experience living cultures and festivals. According to the United Nations World Tourism Organization (UNWTO) approximately 1,235 million international trips were made for the purposes of tourism worldwide in 2016; 25% or 309 million of these were made in the Asia Pacific region. Tourism in the post-war modern era has continued to grow and expand its attainability so that it is now regarded by many economies around the world as a major driver for growth and development. Indeed, the UNWTO characterises an average 6.5% growth in tourist arrivals since 1950 "as one of the most remarkable economic and social phenomena of the past century". And at an average of 13% during this period, such phenomenal growth has nowhere been stronger than in the Asia Pacific.

Modern attempts to define heritage tourism tend to focus on its use of a heritage asset or assets, usually tangible but possibly supplemented by intangible elements, as the focus for the tourist experience (Timothy, 2011). Whereas cultural tourism is tourism with a purpose to experience another culture, heritage tourism (by virtue of the way it has developed) carries overtones of tourism for the purpose of conservation (however successfully this may have been achieved or managed). Smith (2009) characterises heritage tourism as being largely concerned with the interpretation and representation of the past and, as such, is a branch of cultural tourism that is a veritable political and ethical minefield. The word "heritage" immediately raises the question of "what have we preserved for the purposes of this tourist visit and why?" It is important to consider exactly who is defining what we frame and construct as heritage worth preserving. As essentially a visual, tangible and material phenomenon aesthetes and experts, connoisseurs and curators have come to dominate the debate on what and what is not "heritage", resulting in a reliance on their associated skills of interpretation, presentation and representation (Waterton and Watson, 2010) in a tourism context. This creates a self-perpetuating and self-referentially circular set of definitions that can risk becoming overbearing orthodoxy.

Heritage tourism contributes hugely to both developed and developing nations in terms of GDP but also by consolidating in the minds of visitors and locals alike a sense of identity and pride. Heritage tourism can be said to be the mechanism by which a nation, city or region's personality is projected; if we were to anthropomorphise such inanimate objects as buildings, streets and artefacts, these would be treasured ambassadors to the world. But who puts words into the mouths of these ambassadors? In tourism terms, historic sites need to be commodified as tourism products (or exploited if you will) to speak. It is this process that determines how the objects of commodification address their audiences which can have great significance for how they are perceived, in turn impacting on such fundamentals as national and local identity. Hall (1999) evocatively states that heritage can be a "powerful mirror"; it reflects back to us who we are locally, nationally and personally, but issues of ownership, authenticity, interpretation and dialectical discourse can mean that we are looking into a distorted mirror that alienates or excludes us.

The role of interpretation in developing heritage assets represents a significant part of the message communication mechanism, whether that be through human guides or the full array of display techniques available to museums (from static graphics to immersive audio-visual). It enables the heritage stewards to educate and entertain through the deployment of various display techniques for storytelling: to convey a lasting meaning and sense of importance through creating an emotional connection with perceived authenticity; raise awareness to help in the conservation effort; allow the targeting of a substantial visitation audience through schools; act as a potential source of revenue; and can be used as a crowd control tool. In other words, it aids "visitability". However, heritage attraction design does not operate in a vacuum and must negotiate the seemingly opposed forces of globalisation and the search for local identity, the practical requirements of conservation and the need for commercial viability.

A review of the literature reveals the dearth of material about the inter-action between the role of interpretation and commodification identified in Howard's (2003) Heritage Process. Timothy (2011) concludes that inter-pretive planning does not just have a storytelling function but has a role to play in protecting the past, adding value and raising funds. He lays out a process for interpretive planning (goals and objectives, situation analysis, data synthesis, recommendations, implementation, evaluation and moni-toring). However, there is no real attempt to put interpretive planning into the context of overall attraction development or illustrate how it might be a strategic tool. Other studies have characterised the strategic role of inter-pretation as underpinning management, marketing, financial decisions and strategies (Millar, 1989), and as having a crucial and central role in sus-tainable tourism in general, as well as effective management of heritage sites through encouraging mindfulness in visitors (Moscardo, 1996).

Whilst the literature on the role of interpretation in the adaptive re-use of heritage sites for tourism purposes is scarce, it seems to be a generally accepted proposition that interpretation plays a key role in the sustainable management and ordering of management priorities. Given the general agreement of its key role amongst commentators who touch on the topic, there is remarkably little analysis of how interpretation might have a more clearly articulated strategic role to play throughout the process of the devel-opment of a heritage tourism product. This study intends to explore how the profile of interpretation and interpretive planning, as an important part of the strategic management of the regeneration process that is the *raison d'etre* of such projects, can be raised in the heritage revitalisation process.

The heritage tourist and consumption

Touted as the world's bestselling travel book and New York Times best-seller, the popularity of "1000 Places to See Before You Die" (Schultz, 2011) reveals a widespread bucket list, train-spotting mentality towards cultural tourism. So, the acquisitive nature of mass cultural tourism makes consumption an appropriate word to use here. The classic image of cul-tural tourism is still closely tied to the European model of middle-class, passive consumption of historic sites and museums (Richards, 2007). A place, a site, a dance, a food does not seem to have been truly experienced until it has been photographed, videoed, posed with, thoroughly gawked at and often replayed to an appreciative group of tourists, all with similar photographs, videos and experiences. However, beneath the sometimes crass manifestation of the desire to possess iconic experiential imagery is a noble idea – to learn (however superficially) about another culture. There are worse things to be doing on holiday.

Tourism, including heritage tourism, is primarily a commercial activity or, more accurately, a collection of activities that involves the consumption of experiences or that provide entertainment (often in the form of learning opportunities). Tribe (2005) counts capital as one of four requirements (including land, labour and technology) necessary for economic and, by extension, tourism growth. In tourism terms, cultural capital is an important resource for a nation, having been invested in and preserved by previous generations. Cultural assets – built, cultural and natural – if realised, marketed and managed properly can act as attractions or demand generators (Bull, 1991; Lew, 1987; McIntosh and Goeldner, 1990; McKercher and du Cros, 2002; Pearce, 1989).

Heritage conservationists bristle at the notion that tourism has somehow rescued heritage that might otherwise have disappeared, fearing presumably the "Disneyfication" or watering down of heritage for the consumption of visitors. Howard (2003) typifies this view: "Heritage has many markets, only one of which is the tourist. The tourist market may have a deep pocket, but much heritage is not designed for them." In his view, the idea that heritage means tourism needs to be resisted. Timothy and Boyd (2003) provide a rather more useful, if self-admittedly reductive, model of heritage and heritage tourism putting the heritage tourism experience at its heart. It attempts to capture how the actual outcome of a heritage visit is influenced and shaped by a mix of elements, chief amongst which is interpretation.

An attraction might be something that has evolved quite organically, such as Cantonese cuisine, but the deliberate creation of attractions enables a more controlled approach to dealing with mass tourism, possibly minimising the impact to the host community, and maximising the experience for the tourists and returns to be potentially ploughed into sustainable practices. The more mainstream the target audience (or "mid-centrics" in Plog parlance), the more controlled the experience needs to be (McKercher and du Cros, 2002). We must, of course, also be careful that we are aware of our characterisation of the tourist as an "all-encompassing, analytical monolith" (Winter *et al.*, 2009), in other words a white, Western male. The weight of academic tourism history from North American and European institutions can sometimes blind us to the local and regional tourists at the doors of our very own attractions. But at the same time, how accurate is it to talk about an archetypal "Asian tourist"?

From a management point of view there are three main classes of heritage assets: buildings and archaeological sites; heritage cities, routes and cultural landscapes; and movable cultural property and museums (McKercher and du Cros, 2002). The visitors themselves, however, do not tend to plan their visit according to these criteria. Looking at it from an attraction-driven visitor perspective, types of heritage tourism might break down into artistic, natural, living cultural, built, industrial, personal or dark heritage (Timothy and Boyd, 2003). Smith (2009) includes military and literary heritage attractions as distinct genres. And there is considerable crossover between what might be seen as heritage and cultural tourism. For instance, is a visit to a museum or viewing a performance in an ancient amphitheatre heritage or cultural tourism? Does it matter?

Tourists, or in this case consumers, use destinations as prisms through which to satisfy socio-psychological needs (Crompton, 1979). These can range from a simple impulse to "get away from it all", a mind-broadening ambition to "see the world", the desire to boast at dinner parties, a Room with a View-like longing for interaction with new social equals, or the postmodern journey to find oneself. These motivations will affect where we choose to go and what we choose to do when we get there. A constant, however, seems to be the desire for the exotic and authentic (MacCannell, 1989), the eternal search for the sacred. Much like secular pilgrims or modern-day homo viator (Swatos and Tomasi, 2002), we can transform a mundane scene for a local person (such as a kiss in a Paris street) into an iconic image embodying an archetype (romance) through the medium of the tourist's gaze (Urry, 1990). It is the tourist industry's role to predict these inspirations and create products to satisfy them in a fast-changing, ever more connected world.

Park and Choi's study (2011) of tourist attitudes to visiting Gyeongbok Palace in South Korea shows that four dimensions affected their satisfaction and post-visit intentions, namely historicity, education, convenience and experience. In particular, historicity influenced their intention to visit, whilst cultural assets, historical buildings and traditional ceremonies affected visitor satisfaction, intention to return and intention to recommend. McKercher and du Cros (2002) suggest five types of cultural tourist – the purposeful tourist (culture is the prime motivator), the sightseer (interested in culture but satisfied with a shallower experience), the serendipitous tourist (stumbling across a deep cultural experience by chance), the casual tourist (weakly motivated and seeking a shallow experience) and the incidental tourist (for whom culture is not a stated motive but who visits nevertheless). As so often a lifestyle and life-stage driven activity, whilst it is useful for the industry to try to analyse the heritage tourism market, sometimes it is better to just appreciate its diversity and dynamism (Smith, 2009).

But who decides what is worth consuming? On the grand scale, the institutional version of the heritage bucket list is UNESCO's world heritage site list that currently comprises of 962 sites – natural (188), cultural (745) and mixed (29) – of "outstanding universal value". This listing, requiring as it does the practices of surveying, recording, documentation and conservation by experts, confers upon these sites a symbolic or cultural capital which, if suitably treated and manipulated, can be converted and commodified into economic value (Bandelj and Wherry, 2011). The amenability to "cultural capitalization" means that heritage is certainly a kind of tourism product. Indeed, not recognising heritage assets as the tourism products they are can lead to a failure to optimise their benefit or, in other words, exploit them properly. Thankfully, in Hong Kong, site managers are often eager to have their sites promoted as tourism products (Ho and McKercher, 2008).

The evolution of interpretation

Commonly, discussions about the discipline of interpretation in tourism or museums begins with a reference to Freeman Tilden's six principles of interpretation (1977) which were intended to reveal "something of the beauty and wonder, the inspiration and spiritual meaning that lie behind what the visitor can with his senses perceive":

1   Any interpretation that does not somehow relate what is being displayed or described to something within the personality or experience of the visitor will be sterile.
2   Information, as such, is not Interpretation. Interpretation is revelation based upon information. But they are entirely different things. However, all interpretation includes information.
3   Interpretation is an art, which combines many arts, whether the materials presented are scientific, historical or architectural. Any art is in some degree teachable.
4   The chief aim of Interpretation is not instruction, but provocation.
5   Interpretation should aim to present a whole rather than a part, and must address itself to the whole man rather than any phase.
6   Interpretation addressed to children (say up to the age of 12) should not be a dilution of the presentation to adults, but should follow a fundamentally different approach. To be at its best it will require a separate program.

These principles reveal a clearly contructivist approach where interpreters of knowledge aim to provoke visitors to build their own understandings rather than expect to teach anything. It should be remembered that these principles were formulated in the United States of 1960s focused on primarily guided interpretation of national parks (Howard, 2003). Tilden has subsequently been criticised, perhaps not entirely fairly, by Staiff (2014) who argues that, rather than institutional gatekeepers revealing meaning intrinsically contained within objects to visitors, meaning is created by the visitor within a cultural and historical frame of reference. However, many institutions and attractions continued to didactically communicate information as a linear deterministic series of objects.

In the 1980s and particularly the 1990s, the museum world in the United Kingdom and United States began to realise that the objects on display in national collections were only talking to aficionados. Too many people were not seeing themselves reflected in the "powerful mirror" of their own heritage. These debates about representation, ownership and access have important implications for their distant cousin the revitalised heritage tourism product. In other words, who's telling the story, whose story are we telling and to whom are we telling it? Vergo (1989) identified the root of the problem as being too much discussion about museum methods and not enough about the purposes of museums.

The key trend in 1980s Britain was a Thatcherite-led reduction in public funding which necessitated museums to find other sources of income such as corporate sponsorship and, increasingly, charging visitors for entry. This commercialisation of museums meant that they were no longer simply repositories and conservators of artefacts but had to reinvent themselves as entertainment commodities in an experience economy. Critics derided the dumbing down of museums and the perceived requirement for them to compete with theme parks.

Throughout the 1980s and '90s, the purpose of museums (and by association heritage visitor centres) was being increasingly redefined by both the people who held the private purse strings and their potential audiences. The shift from an object-based curatorial-focused approach to a more visitor-centric philosophy meant that new methods of developing museums were needed. And this was not just a UK, US or even European phenomenon; rising economies such as Taiwan embarked on ambitious programmes of museum building. Many of these new museums had no objects at all (being about science or natural science) and so new techniques of storytelling, interpretive planning and designing for museums evolved. As few museums had their own design departments (or in the case of new museums often lacked even a curatorial department), this emerging aspect of the experience economy gave rise to a new wave of creative professionals in the niche specialist 3-dimensional interior design category of museum design.

In the UK, this process was only accelerated by money made available for large-scale visitor centres around the country by the Lottery Fund through the Millennium Commission on a variety of topics from pop music to digital art. The highpoint (or nadir depending on your viewpoint) was the Millennium Dome which, despite overwhelmingly negative media coverage, was surprisingly well visited. Not all of these projects were a success for a wide range of reasons. Half the battle for these institutions was to actually realise that they were a tourism product; failure to understand this in heritage tourism development leads to a lack of understanding of market demand, a lack of asset evaluation, a lack of clearly defined management objectives and priorities, and the isolation of product development (Ho and McKercher, 2008). It is arguable that interpretive planning and interpretation are integral to each of these factors. Indeed, "presentation, interpretation and verification has a direct bearing on motivations to visit and engage with heritage tourism sites" (Bryce *et al.*, 2015).

It is against this background that the role of interpretive planning within the heritage tourism product development process continues to evolve.

The heritage tourism product development process

It is hard to know which came first – the increasing demand for heritage attractions (sites, museums, visitor centres etc.) or the increasing number of such attractions. Certainly, the public money spent on such attractions in many major tourism destination cities has seen steady increase in the past couple of decades, particularly in European destinations as they vie with neighbours for increased tourist traffic both from within the EU and from outside (notably China). And the competition is not just between countries but between towns and cities. Economies of differing scales that rely heavily on tourism have been exposed to growing competition and demands for greater investment in their attractions offer. Hong Kong has been no exception to that. Satisfying this demand has often led to a production-led (rather than a consumption-led) approach with the "creative industries" being seen as vital to underpin the cultural development of urban areas (Richards, 2001).

We can look at the process of developing a heritage tourism product from two key perspectives – the processing of heritage itself and the way in which the attractions industry goes about creating a tourism product. According to Howard (2003), the heritage process (Figure 1.1) begins with selecting and forming what constitutes heritage through to eventual old age, loss and destruction. In terms of the origination of heritage, art (fine, contemporary, music, certain architecture) is generally regarded as "born heritage" and he makes an interesting comparison between the subjective heritage distinction that librarians apply to whether to shelve a book under "literature" or "fiction". Achieving heritage status usually relies on longevity, surviving the longest, so acquiring the cachet of obsolescence

Figure 1.1 Howard's model of the life cycle of heritage.

and possibly eventual rarity. Acquisition is the "thrusting upon" objects or sites of the status of heritage through their association with a famous person or event. This can often be a part of the process in which independent hobbyists or academics have much to do with establishing the provenance of an artefact or collection.

Once accepted as heritage, the stage of inventory-making might involve creating a catalogue or classification system. Inventory and designation may go hand-in-hand or closely follow and usually requires a panel of experts or a recognised advisory body such a UNESCO or English Heritage. Once its status and cultural value has been established and officially endorsed (bearing in mind the implication for local, regional and national cultural identity that brings with it the promotion or demotion of certain narratives), a process of protection is set in place which might involve legislation but more commonly relates to repair, restoration or conservation (the intangible equivalent is re-enactment such as playing a piece of music with original instruments).

Commodification is the mechanism by which visitors are attracted to view the object. Indeed, it may be necessary to make this a commercial transaction in order to financially support the retention and ongoing maintenance of the heritage itself. The end of the process resists the optimism of most cyclical models and allows for the probable reality of loss and destruction of heritage that we have all witnessed or mourned. The point of commodification is the focus of this study and involves the interaction between interpretation and the commodification of the heritage object. It is here that tourism is an essential driver to the commodification process; while theories of museology and attraction design tend to drive the approach to interpretation. Howard (2003) quite properly assigns interpretation a prominent position in this model but curiously does not elaborate in detail about how the interaction between this and the commodification process suggested by the two-way arrows in Figure 1.1 actually works. In diagrammatic terms, its prominence suggests an essential, strategic role in both driving the process of commodification as well as being acted upon by it. Nor, significantly, does he include within the description of renovation any reference to revitalisation as an option for a heritage site, suggesting just what a relatively new field this is.

As previously stated, Timothy (2011) says that "interpretation is a valuable management tool", but he provides little written evidence of the strategic nature of the role of interpretation in the development of visitor attractions (including those based on heritage). Whilst he covers the role of interpretation in educating and entertaining visitors, preservation/ conservation, crowd management, income generation and the various tools and techniques, he does not put interpretation into the context of the overall development of a visitor attraction nor how it might strategically interact with key players and consultants (such as architects) in the process. Interpretive planning is very much couched simply in terms of a standalone process at the front-end of a project to produce a set of guidelines primarily for storytelling that are then monitored.

A significant contribution to the somewhat meagre literature on how to develop a visitor attraction is Swarbrooke (2002). By visitor attractions, he primarily means theme parks, museums, heritage buildings, and natural landscapes which also act as tourist products. In an extensive section on the development process, and especially the design of visitor attractions, interpretation is not mentioned (surprisingly not even in the context of storytelling).

The role of interpretation in urban heritage revitalisation projects

"Through interpretation, understanding; through understanding, appreciation; through appreciation, protection."

(1950s US National Park Service manual as quoted by Freeman Tilden (1977))

There have traditionally been two main roles ascribed to interpretation – education and entertainment (Timothy, 2011). The "irrefutable" educative role (Timothy and Boyd, 2003) can be both formal in terms of outreach programmes to schools, as well as informal since people learn from the experience of their visits. Entertainment is seen as a way of competing with other calls on the attention of the visiting public, as well as sugaring the pill of institutional messaging. For instance, Cheung (2008) points to the success of the range of interpretive devices and presentations in attracting, particularly domestic, tourists to the Hong Kong Wetland Park, in order to promote both ecotourism and raise awareness of the need for wetland conservation. However, he does not speak to the role of interpretation in the development process of these projects in order to achieve the outcomes of education and entertainment. As previously mentioned, Moscardo (1996) proposes that interpretation can promote a sense of "mindfulness" in visitors that can have a significant effect on the attitude to conservation on the site itself.

Timothy (2011) further states that "interpretation is one of the most vital elements of sustainable management at heritage properties.... Effectual interpretive planning is essential". It stands to reason, therefore, that interpretive planning must have a strategically important role in the development of such projects. McIntosh (1999) places the visitor experience at the heart of the heritage management process. Millar (1989) ranks the importance of interpretive planning to management even more strongly when she says that heritage interpretation is the key to a successful management policy for heritage sites and is central to the management process. As well as teaching us about our past, it should act as a starting point that enables the designation of management priorities, underpinning management, marketing and financial decisions and strategies.

Creating a sense of place and place identity is another important role ascribed to interpretation by Uzzell (1996). Indeed, place itself can be seen to be a key theoretical dimension by which to evaluate interpretation as it "captures, in an holistic way, the inter-relationships, complexities and variabilities between visitors, their experience and the site that is being interpreted" (Stewart and Kirby, 1998). Fulfilling tourism experiences of heritage buildings have been seen to have three mains themes: "visual appeal", "personal reflections" and "engaging experiences" (Willson and McIntosh, 2007). Interpretation is intrinsic to the latter aspect. Hems and Blockley (2006) present a series of perspectives on heritage interpretation in the British context and how we can meet the challenge of ascribing value to a place, how we choose which stories to tell and how this impacts on the significance of the place whose stories we relate. They very much value the visitor as part of the interpretive process to bring "real life into buildings from the past" rather than being guided by the old adage of "bringing the past to life".

In an Asian context, telling the story of Singapore's wartime occupation under the Japanese through conservation and interpretation is seen to serve important aims of nation building and have a social, economic and political value (Henderson, 2007). Teo and Chang (2009) point out how the revitalisation of buildings from the colonial period in Singapore is catching the new waves of hybridity, eclecticism and nostalgia in the region. Local communities, such as that in Toraja, South Sulawesi Indonesia, can themselves see the benefit of interpretation to "convey local wisdom to enhance the visitor experience" (Kausar and Gunawan, 2017). Even more than this, in the context of contested histories, heritage "can be a safe and neutral ground for mediating political contentions and conflicts" (Park, 2011). Nor should we forget that interpretation is not static; it evolves over time. Weiner's (1998) study of Walt Disney's Carousel of Progress examined the way the interpretation of the collective memory of family life changed between 1967 and 1995. Despite the persistent nostalgia for an idealised view of family life, there were significant changes in the representation of the roles within the family. This is important because, according to Wallace (1989), "Walt Disney has taught people more history, in a more memorable way, than they ever learned at school" – possibly 100 million people in its first two decades.

By no means everyone in the heritage field is convinced that more interpretation is necessarily better interpretation. Howard (2003) argues that there are three cases against this: curatorial (attracting more people means potentially more destruction of heritage sites), communications (proposing necessarily limited storylines is a limiting factor) and cultural (a little knowledge is a dangerous thing). The building of meaning in a relatively sophisticated audience is a complex process which involves aspects such as communication theory, passive/active audience transmission models, constructivism and semiotics, consumer theory, ideas of selective reading, and cultural capital (Mason, 2005). Copeland (2006) provides a theoretical framework to explain the way that meaning is constructed on archaeological sites and suggests strategies for interpretation: presenting the site with an emphasis on big concepts (such as justice); relying heavily on evidence; treating visitors as thinkers with emerging ideas about the past; mediating the historic environment; valuing exploration; encouraging discourse; assessing and evaluating to improve interpretation.

How does the literature deal with interpretive planning's place in the overall heritage attraction development process? In as much as this can be compared to exhibition design, Hughes (2010) divides responsibilities between client and design manager as follows (with addition of asterisks which will be explained below). Under client responsibilities he lists Planning (Concept*, Exhibit curation*, Content research*, Sales & marketing, Audience research*, Branding*, Outreach*, Accessibility, Education*, Facilities*, Press/PR) and Logistics (Content co-ordination*, Security, Staff training*, Conservation*, Computing, Exhibit installation, Shipping/ logistics, Audio-visual maintenance, Health & safety, Planning consent, Maintenance). For the design manager he lists Design (Narrative design*, Scriptwriting*, 3-D design*, Graphic design*, Artworking*, Technical drawings, Film concept*, Interactive design*, Sound design*, Software design*, Product specification) and Realisation (Construction, Graphic production, Lighting installation, Audio-visual installation, Mechanical and electrical, Modelmaking, Specialist trades, Flooring, Repairs to building fabric, Film production).

However, Hughes only mentions interpretation in terms of the development of the storyline, once again consigning it to just narrative storytelling. From a professional point of view, I would say that interpretive planning and interpretation straddle both the client and design manager's responsibilities and is key to nearly half the tasks in Hughes' list (ascribed an asterisk above). Black (2001) regards heritage interpretation as "the essential basis for quality in the development of the concept" of an attraction through providing an emphasis on the site or collection, making connections with the visitor, encouraging active visitor participation and social interaction, impacting on the senses and emotions, overlaying a thematic approach, opening the display media tool box, and making it a fun but at the same time structured learning experience.

What does an interpretive plan contain? Lord and Lord (2009), long-term professionals in the field of museum planning, list the components of an interpretive plan for a museum as:

• Objectives of the exhibition
• Intended visitor experience
• Levels of interpretation (for different age groups)
• Component-by-component description of the exhibition, including:

    • Communication objectives of each component
    • Means of expression to communicate these objectives
    • Diagrams of visitor flow patterns
    • Initial concept sketches

These are fundamental aspects that will guide the success or failure of the entire museum and the interpretive planner will often have a role to play (either on the consultant or client side) in overseeing the implementation of the spirit of the interpretive plan throughout the process of the heritage attraction design and fabrication.

The historic narratives associated with a site are often the *raison d'etre* for preservation and the development of a tourism product. Indeed, in an urban context, in the absence of much surviving material culture other than a building, ruin or remains, the intangible story may be all we have left to play with. However, despite lip service being paid to the importance of interpretation and interpretive planning to the visitor experience and long-term sustainability of a heritage attraction, there has been remarkably little written about how interpretation contributes strategically to the development and ongoing management of attraction. This study is an exploratory attempt to bridge some of those gaps.

References

Adams, C. and Roy, J. eds (2007). *Travel, geography and culture in Ancient Greece, Egypt and the Near East*, Oxford: Oxbow.

Bandelj, N. and Wherry, F. (2011). *The cultural wealth of nations*, Stanford: Stanford University Press.

Beaman, J. (1974). "Distance and the reaction to distance as a function of distance". *Journal of Leisure Research*, 6 (Summer): 220–231.

Black, G. (2001). "Hows of concept design". In *Quality issues in heritage visitor attractions*, edited by Drummond, S. and Yeoman, I. Oxford: Butterworth-Heinemann.

Bryce, D., Curran, R., O'Gorman, K. and Taheri, B. (2015). "Visitors' engagement and authenticity: Japanese heritage consumption". *Tourism Management* 46: 571–581.

Bull, A. (1991). *The economics of travel and tourism*, Melbourne: Pitman

Butler, R. (1980). "The Concept of Tourism Area Cycle of Evolution: the implications for management of resources". *The Canadian Geographer* 24: 5–12.

Cheung, S. (2008). "Wetland tourism in Hong Kong: from birdwatcher to mass Ecotourist". In *Asian Tourism: Growth and Change*, by Cochrane, J. Oxford; Amsterdam: Elsevier.

Copeland, T. (2006). "Constructing pasts: interpreting the historic environment". In *Heritage interpretation*, by Hems, A. and Blockley, M. Abingdon: Routledge.

Crompton, J. (1979). "Motivations for pleasure vacation". *Annals of Tourism Research*, 6(4): 408–424.

Hall, M. (1995). *Introduction to tourism*. Melbourne: Longman.

Hall, S. (1999). *Whose heritage?* Conference, UK: Arts Council.

Hems, A. and Blockley, M. (2006). *Heritage interpretation*. Abingdon, New York: Routledge.

Henderson, J. (2007). "Remembering the Second World War in Singapore: wartime heritage as a visitor attraction". *Journal of Heritage Tourism* 2(1): 36–52.

Ho, P. and McKercher, B. (2008). "Managing heritage resources as tourism products". In *Cultural and heritage tourism in Asia and the Pacific*, edited by Prideaux, B., Timothy, D. and Chon, K. London: Routledge.

Holloway, J.C. (2009). *The business of tourism*. Harlow: Pearson Education.

Howard, P. (2003). *Heritage: management, interpretation, identity*. London: Continuum.

Hughes, P. (2010). *Exhibition design*. London: Laurence King.

Kausar, D. and Gunawan, M. (2017). "Managing heritage tourism in Toraja: strengthening local values and improving tourists' experiences". *Journal of Heritage Tourism*, DOI: 10.1080/1743873X.2017.1411356.

Lehr, J. and Katz, Y. (2003). "Heritage interpretation and politics in Kfar Etzion, Israel". *International Journal of Heritage Tourism* 9(3): 215–228.

Leiper, N. (1995). *Tourism management*. Melbourne: RMIT Press.

Lew, A. (1987). "A framework of tourist attractions research". *Annals of Tourism Research* 14: 553–575.

Lew, A. and McKercher, B. (2006). "Modeling tourist movement: a local destination analysis". *Annals of Tourism Research* 33(2): 403–423.

Lord, G. and Lord, B. (2009). *The manual of museum management*, Lanham: Altamira.

MacCannell, D. (1989). *The tourist*. London: Macmillan.

Mason, R. (2005). "Museums, galleries and heritage: sites of meaning-making and communication". In *Heritage, museums and galleries: an introductory reader*, edited by Corsane, G. Abingdon: Routledge.

McIntosh, A. (1999). "Into the tourist's mind: understanding the value of the heritage Experience". *Journal of Travel and Tourism Marketing* 8: 41–64.

McIntosh, R. and Goeldner, C. (1990). *Tourism: principles, practices, philosophies*. Toronto: John Wiley and Sons.

McKean, J., Johnson, D. and Walsh, R. (1995). "Valuing time in travel cost demand analysis: An empirical investigation". *Land Economics* 71(1): 96–105.

McKercher, B. (1998a). "The effect of distance decay on visitor mix at coastal destinations". *Pacific Tourism Review* 2(3/4): 215–224.

McKercher, B. (1998b). "The effect of market access on destination choice". *Journal of Travel Research* 37: 39–47.

McKercher, B. and du Cros, H. (2002). *Cultural tourism: the partnership between tourism and cultural heritage management*. New York: Routledge.

McKercher, B. and Lew, A. (2003). "Distance decay and the impact of effective tourism exclusion zones on international travel flows". *Journal of Travel Research* 42(2): 159–165.

Mill, R. and Morrison, A. (1985). *The tourism system: an introductory text*. New Jersey: Prentice Hall.

Millar, S. (1989). "Heritage management for heritage tourism". *Tourism Management*, March: 9–14.

Moscardo, G. (1996). "Mindful visitors: heritage and tourism". *Annals of Tourism Research* 23: 376–397.

Moutinho, L. (2001). "Consumer behaviour". *Tourism European Journal of Marketing* 21(10): 5–44.

Oxford Economics (2016). *The impact of heritage tourism on the UK economy*. London: Heritage Lottery Fund.

Park, E. and Choi, B. (2011). "Attractiveness of Gyeongbok Palace as a cultural heritage site". In *Sustainability of tourism: cultural and environmental perspectives* edited by Kozak, M. and Kozak, N., Newcastle Upon Tyne: Cambridge Scholars Publishing.

Park, H. (2011). "Shared national memory as intangible heritage: re-imagining two Koreas as one nation". *Annals of Tourism Research* 38(2): 520–539.

Pearce, D. (1989). *Tourist development*. Harlow: Longman.

Plog, S. (1974). "Why destination areas rise and fall in popularity". *The Cornell H.R.A. Quarterly*, February, 55–58.

Plog, S. (2001). "Why destination areas rise and fall in popularity: an update of a Cornell Quarterly Classic. *Cornell Hotel and Restaurant Quarterly* 42(3): 13–24.

Richards, G. ed. (2001). *Cultural attractions and European tourism*. Walling-ford: CABI.

Richards, G. (2002). "Tourism attraction systems: exploring cultural behaviour". *Annals of Tourism Research* 29(4): 1048–1064.

Richards, G. ed. (2007). *Cultural tourism: global and local perspectives*. New York: Haworth Hospitality Press.

Schultz, P. (2011). *1000 places to see before you die*. New York: Workman.

Smith, M. (2009). *Issues in cultural tourism studies*. London: Routledge.

Staiff, R. (2014). *Re-imagining heritage interpretation: enchanting the past-future*. Farnham: Ashgate.

Stewart, E. and Kirby, V. (1998). "Interpretive evaluation: towards a place approach". *International Journal of Heritage Interpretation* 4 (1): 30–44.

Swatos, W.H. and Tomasi, L. (2002). *From medieval pilgrimage to religious tourism: the social and cultural economics of piety*. Westport: Praeger.

Teo, P. and Chang, T. (2009). "Singapore's postcolonial landscape: boutique hotels as agents". In *Asia on tour: exploring the rise of Asian tourism*, by Winter, T., Teo, P. and Chang, T. (2009). London, New York: Routledge.

Tilden, F. (1977). *Interpreting our heritage*. Chapel Hill: University of North Carolina Press.

Timothy, D.J. (2011). *Cultural and heritage tourism*. Bristol: Channel View.

Timothy, D.J. and Boyd, S.W. (2003). *Heritage tourism*. Harlow: Pearson Education.

Tribe, J. (2005). *The economics of recreation, leisure and tourism*, Oxford: Butterworth-Heinemann.

Urry, J. (1990). *The tourist gaze*. London: Sage.

Uzzell, D. (1996). "Creating place identity through heritage interpretation". *International Journal of Heritage Studies* 1(4): 219–228.

Vergo, P. (1989). *The new museology*, London: Reaktion.

Wallace, M. (1989). "Mickey Mouse history: portraying the past at Disney World". In *History museums in the United States: a critical assessment*, by Leon, W. and Rosenzweig, R. Urbana: University of Illinois Press.

Waterton, E. and Watson, S. (2010). *Culture, heritage and representation*, Farnham: Ashgate.

Weiner, L. (1998). "There's a great big beautiful tomorrow: historic memory and gender in Walt Disney's Carousel of Progress". In *Travel culture: essays on what make us go*, by Williams, C. (1998). Westport, CT: Praeger.

Willson, G. and McIntosh, A. (2007). "Heritage buildings and tourism: an experiential view". *Journal of Heritage Tourism* 2(2): 75–93.

Winter, T., Teo, P. and Chang, T. (2009). *Asia on tour: exploring the rise of Asian Tourism*. London, New York: Routledge.

Zueglow, E. (2016). *A history of modern tourism*. London: Palgrave.

2 Heritage revitalisation for tourism in Hong Kong

Mass tourism has risen since the 1950s to become an important pillar of the Hong Kong economy, and cultural tourism has been integral to this phenomenon. The Hong Kong Tourist Association (HKTA) was set up in 1957 and became the Hong Kong Tourism Board (HKTB) in 2001. Promotional campaigns that have highlighted both natural and cultural heritage assets in Hong Kong include "Wonders never cease" (1995) and "We are Hong Kong, City of Life" (1998). Early evidence of the realisation of the need to develop cultural heritage assets was the creation of the Ping Shan Trail in 1993, and soon afterwards the Central, Western and Lung Yeuk Tau Heritage Trails (Cheung, 2008).

When does demand for more heritage attractions manifest itself in a society? According to Brokensha and Guldberg (1992) and Konrad (1982) some of the prerequisites are an increasing awareness of heritage, an ability to express individuality, greater economic affluence, increased leisure time, mobility, access to the arts, and the need to seek transcendent experiences. It is arguable that these conditions exist in Hong Kong to a greater extent than in previous eras due to a congruence of factors including a greater sense of urgency, particularly amongst the so-called "post-80s" generation, to take advantage of the "two systems" to define a uniquely post-Handover cultural identity for Hong Kong before absorption into China's "one country" in 2047. Hong Kong is now a mature tourism destination with well-established tourism attractions but not a great number of heritage assets compared to other global cities (Ho and McKercher, 2008). A burgeoning interest in the arts has been fuelled by a buoyant Chinese contemporary art market and with the accompanying government capital investment in arts infrastructure such as the much-delayed West Kowloon Cultural District; every new major cultural initiative in Hong Kong these days seems to call itself an "arts hub".

Observers of Hong Kong society often point to the apparent dichotomies and contradictions that lie within the cultural identity of the city. It is a decolonised territory not entirely comfortable with a return to the "motherland", a Chinese city which is on the front of line of the battle between Cantonese and Mandarin dialects where English is widely spoken, and a somewhat democratic administration allied to an autocratic system. In her study of Hong Kong culture and its relationship with identity and tourism, Henderson (2001) refers to the "puzzle" of Hong Kong's cultural identity being unlikely to be solved anytime soon. Nearly two decades later, the puzzle seems to be ever more complex. Given the clear and deep divisions in Hong Kong society about its own cultural identity, what impact does this have on the way that it projects its image to the outside world? The Hong Kong government's statements in relation to the issues of national education and concerns about a growing antipathy towards greater cultural integration with China might lead one to believe that it would position Hong Kong's identity firmly anchored to that of the Motherland. However, when we look at the government branding of Hong Kong (which goes as far back as 2001) the surprising fact is that there is so little or even no reference to China. The strapline for Brand Hong Kong, which also serves for tourism promotion, is "Asia's World City". No mention of China; it locates itself firmly as a cosmopolitan city in Asia, a connected go-between linking Asia and the globe. Amongst the core values, "Free" ("Hong Kong is an open society, where economic and social freedoms are cherished") seems a deliberate attempt to differentiate itself from its more autocratic neighbour. Indeed, in the three paragraphs of brand overview on the government website China is not mentioned once. Yet, despite an evolving sense of self-identity, tourists seem to have a pretty clear idea that Hong Kong is worth experiencing as a physical, cultural and social phenomenon.

In 2017, Hong Kong received over 56 million tourist arrivals, making it the world's most visited city. It is regarded by the Hong Kong SAR Government as a major pillar of the economy, directly contributing 4.5% to GDP in 2017 and indirectly comprising 14.5% of the workforce. The Hong Kong Tourist Board (HKTB) figures look across a range of activities places visited and activities consumed by visitors to Hong Kong. Two studies by McKercher *et al.* (2002) and McKercher (2002) found that 33% of tourists took part in cultural tourism activities, with most of them looking for a shallow understanding of Hong Kong's cultural heritage. However, Hong Kong is facing a considerable amount of competition for both international and domestic visitors from Macau and China.

The HKTB's primary online promotion tool is the Discover Hong Kong website (www.discoverhongkong.com) whose main navigation tabs cover See & Do, Dine & Drink, Shopping, Accommodation, Plan Your Trip and Beyond Hong Kong. Under the Things To Do tab are listed:

- Hong Kong Neighbourhoods (e.g. the newly branded Old Town Central)
- Highlight Attractions (e.g. Top 10: Avenue of Stars, The Peak, Ladies' Market, Clock Tower, Hong Kong Disneyland, Tsim Sha Tsui Promenade, Ocean Park, Temple Street Night Market, Golden Bauhinia Square, and Lan Kwai Fong)
- Events and Festivals (e.g. the Dragon Boat Carnival)
- Arts and Performance (e.g. Arts Museums)
- Culture and Heritage (see below for more details)
- Great Outdoors (e.g. the Hong Kong Wetland Park)
- Tours and Walks (guided and self-guided trails)

Under Culture and Heritage the website lists the following categories:

- Chinese Temples
- Other Places of Worship
- Chinese Festivals
- Declared Monuments
- Historical Sites
- Living Culture
- Modern Architecture
- Museums

In terms of heritage revitalisation projects, the most relevant category is Historical Sites that lists, under separate headings of Chinese and Colonial, 39 sites that "tell the story of Hong Kong's journey from a far-flung outpost of Imperial China to the culturally diverse crossroads of a shrinking world". Of these, projects which represent some form of adaptive re-use of a heritage asset with a serious intention to interpret the site's history and incorporate a substantial amount of commercial use include 1881 Heritage, PMQ, Murray House and the Former Central Police Station Compound.

The development of heritage conservation in Hong Kong

A measure of how far the study of heritage conservation and tourism in Hong Kong has come is the fact that The University of Hong Kong's *25 years of social development in Hong Kong* (Leung and Wong, 1994) does not dedicate a single chapter of its 31 sections to either topic. It is hard to imagine a similar publication being written today covering the last 25 years omitting either subject or indeed the connection between them.

Every year the Hong Kong government publishes a Yearbook that provides a comprehensive review of all government activities across the public realm. A survey of the Hong Kong Yearbooks from the early 1960s gives us the official version of the activities and achievements of the previous year, but it also helps shed light on the priorities and concerns of the time.

The 1960s

In the early 1960s, the Hong Kong government's activity in the field of heritage was minimal, largely consisting of "assistance of various kinds" to the Royal Asiatic Society, an organisation originally founded in Hong Kong in 1847 and revived in 1959 "to encourage an active interest in East Asia, and in Hong Kong in particular". The late 1960s saw increased activity focused on bolstering the ethnographic collections of the City Museum and Art Gallery at City Hall and archaeological digs by the Museum staff and the Archaeological Society.

The 1970s

The unearthed fruits of these labours began to require a more systematic approach to heritage conservation and by the early 1970s the need for heritage conservation legislation was realised, culminating in the Antiquities and Monuments Ordinance (Cap. 53). This was originally drawn up in 1971 and enacted on 1st January 1976 to "provide for the preservation of objects of historical, archaeological and palaeontological interest and for matters ancillary thereto or connected therewith". The Antiquities Advisory Board (AAB) and the Antiquities and Monuments Office (AMO) were established in the same year to oversee the administering of the A&M Ordinance. Cheung (2003) ascribes the start of the process to package a unique heritage distinct from both Mainland China and colonial British Hong Kong to these events.

The first significant mention of the Antiquities and Monuments Section (AMS) comes in the 1978 Yearbook in which its work is described as "such matters as processing licenses to excavate and search for antiquities and the protection of monuments" (HKGIS, 1978). The pace and extent of preservation activity picks ups significantly in the late 1970s, particularly with action to preserve and record prehistoric rock carvings and the restoration of a Han tomb which re-opened as the Lei Cheng Uk Branch Museum in 1978. By 1979, eight historic sites had been declared monuments with conservation work beginning at many of them, including the fort at Tung Chung, ancient kilns on Lantau and the fort ruins on the island of Tung Lung.

The 1980s

The early 1980s saw progress on projects already initiated, such as historic buildings to boundary stones being documented, photographed and recorded on maps, significant progress on the restoration of forts at Tung Chung on Lantau and Tung Long Islands, and a territory-wide archaeology survey directed by the Museum of History and the AMS in 1981. A major amendment of the A&M Ordinance was made in 1982 that allowed government to provide immediate protection for proposed monuments on a temporary basis while the merits of the case were being considered. This considerable step forward made it

> an offence to damage, destroy or make any alteration to a proposed monument without the permission of the Director of Urban Services who may, with the approval of the Governor, declare any place, building, site or structure to be a monument by reason of its historical, archaeological or paleontological significance.
>
> (HKGIS, 1983)

By this time, the number of declared monuments had reached 19 and included the steps and gas lamps of Duddell Street, Central, and the District Office North Building in Tai Po. The intent to restore and open historic sites of indigenous cultural interest to the public was signalled by such initiatives as the restoration of the typical Hakka village of Sheung Yiu Village in Sai Kung.

Prior to the vogue for the designation of heritage sites prompted by the mid-80s' UNESCO World Heritage Convention, Cheung (1999) suggests that most heritage in Hong Kong was regarded as pre-colonial but that subsequently a narrative of "a fishing village turned modern metropolis [was] replaced through the construction of a heritage with distinctive Chinese traditional characteristics".

A greater attempt to involve the public in the process of heritage conservation began in 1986 with the first joint government-community restoration projects at Man Shek Tong (the Liu Clan Ancestral Hall), Sheung Shui, and the Man Mo Temple at Tai Po Market, as well as the appointment of members of the general public to the AAB. 1987 saw a major reorganisation of the AAB to have an appointed chairman with 13 members drawn from a variety of disciplines such as archaeology, history, architecture, anthropology and geology. The number of members of the AAB has subsequently fluctuated on a yearly basis.

Whilst much of the early work on heritage documentation in Hong Kong had been focused on prehistoric archaeology, the growing emphasis on the preservation of built heritage was signalled by the formation of two sub-committees – one for historical buildings and structures, and the other for archaeology and palaeontology. The 1989 Yearbook states that the preserved monument list had risen to 33 and then goes on to make a very direct admission: "Many feel this to be too little, too late and that far more should have been preserved from the wreckers' hammers, including some fine old colonial buildings" (HKGIS, 1989). The following year an increasing emphasis on public communication was underlined by the setting up of a third sub-committee to handle education and publicity. Also in 1989, comes the first mention of an AMO initiative specifically linked to urban renewal schemes with a survey of pre-war buildings in the Central and Western, Wan Chai, Mong Kok, Yau Ma Tei and Kwun Tong districts by the Land Development Corporation.

The 1990s

The early 1990s was characterised by a growing realisation in government of the importance of heritage preservation beyond pre-colonial archaeological sites and built heritage, as well as a widening of historical grading to buildings such as fire stations, hospitals and pre-war schools. The first reference to an official acknowledgement of growing public awareness of the importance of Hong Kong's cultural and historical heritage is made in the 1991 Yearbook which it says is "reflected in the activities of the museums run by the Urban and Regional Councils, and the work of the Antiquities Advisory Board as well as the Antiquities and Monuments Office". In particular, this work included the operating of branch heritage sites by the Hong Kong Museum of History, such as the Law Uk Folk Museum which incorporates a restored village house over 200 years old, the recording of fast disappearing rural villages by the Regional Council, and raising public awareness through exhibitions, guided tours, publications and local studies. More significant, perhaps, is the clear realisation that the public were concerned with colonial-era built heritage with the gazetting as monuments of buildings such as the Wan Chai Post Office, the Old Pathological Institute, the former Western Market and the former Kowloon-Canton Railway Terminus Clock Tower in 1990. In 1991, a major survey of the military graves and monuments of the Hong Kong Cemetery in Happy Valley signified an important recognition of the need to be able to tell the stories of the lives of ordinary former citizens of Hong Kong through heritage conservation, in this case the servicemen, civil servants and their dependents who died in the early years of the city. The AMO also found a permanent home this year at the restored former British School in Tsim Sha Tsui, which enabled them to house a resource centre

on heritage preservation, resulting in increased public promotion activity
in 1992 and the hosting of two conferences – The Future of Hong Kong's
Past and In Search of Times Past – to discuss the principles and techniques
of building conservation.

The establishment in 1992 of the Lord Wilson Heritage Trust, named
after the former governor, was a major step forward in providing a focus

Figure 2.1 The Ping Shan Heritage Trail: inaugurated in December 1993 was the
first of its kind in Hong Kong.

for community activity on heritage preservation, as well as an additional source of funding for heritage protection and promotion which had previously relied heavily on the Royal Hong Kong Jockey Club. The funding bore its first significant fruit with the opening of the inaugural heritage trail in Hong Kong at Ping Shan, Yuen Long in 1994. This was a significant development in the beginnings of a conscious effort on the part of the government to link heritage with tourism (both domestic and foreign) and is, as Cheung (1999) states, a manifestation of the construction of an emerging Hong Kong identity. The years prior to the handover also saw the pace of archaeological survey and investigation forced to pick up in order to work ahead of major infrastructure projects such as the new airport at Chek Lap Kok.

The 1997 handover of sovereignty from Britain to the People's Republic of China obviously represented a pivotal moment in the history of Hong Kong's heritage policies. The aptly named Hong Kong – A New Era (HKGIS, 1997) records an important development in heritage policy cooperation with the Hong Kong Exposition in Beijing, which was organised by the Hong Kong and Macau Affairs Office of the State Council of the People's Republic of China and the Xinhua News Agency – Hong Kong Branch. This would have been highly unlikely under the British colonial administration. Cross-border cooperation with such bodies as the Guangdong Institute of Cultural Relics and Archaeology, the Anthropology Department of Zhongshan University, the Guangxi Provincial Archaeological Team and the Hunan Institute of Cultural Relics and Archaeology continued and gathered pace from the late 1990s onwards.

The enactment in 1998 of the Environmental Impact Assessment (EIA) Ordinance created a formal framework and regulatory process to "identify any negative impacts on sites of cultural heritage and to propose measures to mitigate these impacts". In the following year, the close relationship between heritage and tourism was recognised by the holding of an international conference called "Heritage and Tourism" jointly organised by the Antiquities Advisory Board, the Lord Wilson Heritage Trust and the AMO.

The 2000s

Further proof of the government's focus on the link between heritage and tourism came in 2000 with the opening of the final phase of the Central and Western Heritage Trail. Between 2001 and 2007, preservation, restoration and development work on a large number of projects included some that have since become synonymous with the image of Hong Kong heritage tourism such as the former Kowloon-Canton Railway Clock Tower, the former Marine Police Headquarters Compound (now known as 1881 Heritage) in Tsim Sha Tsui, and the Central Police Station Compound on Hollywood Road.

In his 2007–2008 Policy Address, the Chief Executive shifted the emphasis from solely preserving built heritage to revitalising it through adaptive re-use, as well as introducing the concept of a district-wide approach in the case of the "open-air bazaar" in Tai Yuen Street and Cross Street, Wan Chai. The 2007 Yearbook bears this out as it affords heritage conservation a more prominent status within the report, promoting it for the first time from a section of the Recreation, Sports and Arts section to having its own section with Infrastructure Development. More importantly, responsibility for heritage conservation policies was transferred from the Home Affairs Bureau to the Works Bureau of the newly formed Development Bureau. And due to the rising public attention paid to heritage conservation, the Bureau adopted a mission statement as follows:

> To protect, conserve and revitalise as appropriate historical and heritage sites and buildings through relevant and sustainable approaches for the benefit and enjoyment of present and future generations. In implementing this policy, due regard will be given to development needs in public interest, respect for private property rights, budgetary considerations, cross-sector collaboration and active engagement of stakeholders and the general public.

It also drew up and formalised a number of initiatives for heritage conservation work (HKGIS, 2007):

a   To require public works projects to conduct heritage impact assessments;
b   To implement revitalisation of historic buildings through partnership schemes;
c   To provide economic incentives for conservation and maintenance of privately-owned historic buildings;
d   To set up the "Commissioner for Heritage's Office"; and
e   To conduct public engagement and publicity programmes

The Bureau began to explore various incentive schemes, such as land exchange and transfer of development rights, to encourage private owners to preserve their historic buildings. More innovative ways of preserving heritage were announced with the "Revitalising Historic Buildings Through Partnership Scheme" which aims to speed up the process of turning government-owned historic buildings into unique cultural landmarks through partnership with NGOs.

The new initiatives in revitalisation moved forward from 2008 with the launch and selection in 2009 of proposals from six non-profit organisations to revitalise six historic buildings – the Old Tai O Police Station, the Fong Yuen Study Hall, Lai Chi Kok Hospital, Lui Seng Chun, Mei Ho House and the North Kowloon Magistracy. Also in 2009, Hong Kong's built heritage assets were further reviewed and graded through a more in-depth survey of 1,444 buildings with higher heritage value selected from the 8,800 surveyed buildings that was carried out by AMO in 2002–2004. A two-tier assessment approach was adopted for the assessment of these buildings with them being scored against six criteria – historical interest, architectural merit, group value, social value and local interest, authenticity and rarity. By the end of October 2011, 160 buildings had been accorded Grade 1 status, 309 buildings Grade 2 status and 440 buildings Grade 3 status.

The 2010s

Two announcements on a single day in December 2012, however, reveal both the new scrutiny under which heritage policy in Hong Kong operates and its limitations. Two long-running disputes involving heritage properties – the plan to redevelop the west wing of the former government headquarters in Central and plans to preserve the historic, privately-owned Ho Tung Gardens – ended in a government climb down and admission of policy failure respectively. In the case of the former, the government bowed to pressure from, amongst others, the specially-formed Government Hill Concern Group and, rather than sell the land for redevelopment, will house the Department for Justice and other international legal organisations. Civic Party leader Alan Leong Kah-wit hailed it as a "victory for civil society" and it certainly represents a major win for built heritage conservation activists in Hong Kong.

In the second case, the government's failure to persuade the owner of the Ho Tung Gardens to turn the property over to public hands revealed the limitations of the Antiquities and Monuments Ordinance in acquiring and preserving properties in private ownership. Following the owner Ho Min-kwan's application in mid-2010 to redevelop the 1927 Peak mansion built by famed Eurasian businessman and philanthropist Robert Ho-tung, the building was declared a Grade I listed historic site by the Antiquities Advisory Board. In January 2011, the government invoked the Antiquities and Monuments Ordinances for only the fourth time in its history, so providing the Gardens with a stay of execution and moratorium on development for a year to allow negotiations to take place. Following the rejection by the owner of all the government proposals, its intention to declare the property a monument that would have put them on a direct collision course with the owner faltered at the last minute as, in the words of Paul Chan Mo-po, Secretary for Development, "We understand that not everyone would agree with spending billions of dollars of public money on private heritage sites." By 2016, eight of the 15 projects approved under the Revitalising Historic Buildings Through Partnership scheme were already operating, costing taxpayers HK$1.7 billion. Given that most of these projects are meant to be self-sustaining after two years, the tension between commercial viability and preservation of history will continue to be tested and their long-term sustainability under scrutiny.

Interpretive planning in Hong Kong heritage revitalisation projects

A review of heritage revitalisation products in Hong Kong developed since the 1970s reveals a wide range of interpretive approaches to the presentation of the city's narrative. It also reveals a range of ambition in terms of the extent to which these attractions sought to present Hong Kong's wider story. There appears to be three main categories of extensiveness relative to each other: high extensiveness where the product has attempted to present a relatively comprehensive, contextualised version of Hong Kong's story; medium extensiveness where the product has attempted to present some contextualised version of Hong Kong's story; and low extensiveness where the product has made little or no attempt to contextualise a version of Hong Kong's story (Table 2.1).

The majority of revitalised heritage products have made little or no effort to provide any content links or contextualisation to a broader Hong Kong historical narrative. This is understandable in the case of some venues such as the Peninsula Hotel or The Pawn that are privately owned hospitality businesses with no obligation to serve the public as a visitor attraction, despite their iconic heritage status in the city, or working places of worship such as St Andrew's Church. Other sites such as the Clock Tower or Duddell Street Gas Lamps have the excuse of being single points of interest in busy urban settings without the opportunity for extensive interpretation in a dedicated facility.

More remarkable, however, are sites that have been specially developed and promoted as heritage tourism products such as the Western Market, Murray House and the Tai O Heritage Hotel. To take the latter as an example; this is the first of a new generation of heritage buildings when, in 2009, the Hong Kong Heritage Conservation Foundation Limited (established by the family behind the property developers Sino Group) was selected to undertake its revitalisation under Batch I of the Development

Table 2.1 Distribution by extensiveness of the presentation of the Hong Kong story in the city's heritage revitalisation products

---

High extensiveness
Hong Kong Heritage Discovery Centre
Dr Sun Yat-sen Museum
Law Uk Folk Museum
Sam Tung Uk Museum

Medium extensiveness
Lei Chung Uk Han Tomb Museum
Ping Shan Tang Clan Museum
The Blue House

Low extensiveness – where the product has made little or no attempt to contextualise a version of Hong Kong's story
1881 Heritage
Clock Tower
Duddell Street Gas lamps
Flagstaff House Tea Museum
Lui Seng Tong
Murray House
The Pawn
Peninsula Hotel
Sheung Yiu Folk Museum
St Andrew's Church
Tai O Heritage Hotel
University of Hong Kong
Wanchai Environmental Resource Centre
Western Market
Yau Ma Tei Theatre

Bureau's Revitalising Historic Buildings Through Partnership Scheme. In 2010, it was graded as a Grade II historic building by the Antiquities Advisory Board. Physical interpretation of the site consists of brass plaques outside each of the rooms to explain their former function. A guided tour is available to explain "the original use of the rooms, the history of the marine guards and the tranquil fishing village" (according to the hotel website). However, little or no attempt is made to provide any permanent interpretation that puts this heritage asset into the context of the wider story of Hong Kong or, indeed, the story of law and order in Hong Kong. The major new built element on the site is a large glazed atrium space at rooftop level used as a restaurant. Another potential space for interpretation (containing former cells) is used as a front management office and retail outlet, with merchandise being displayed in the cells themselves. To be fair, the project is primarily a hospitality venue with limited space for display and it is a recipient of a UNESCO award which may be largely ascribed to its work with the Tai O local community. 1881 Heritage takes a similar approach with individual elements of the site described in terms of its architectural/historical value by brass panels (that break almost every rule of good practice for public exhibition graphics), but with little contextual information. This is despite having considerably more room than the Tai O Heritage Hotel in which to provide such a narrative including a dedicated exhibition gallery. This is, alas, primarily used to promote the developer Cheung Kong's role in the revitalisation of the site through a video presentation.

Both of the heritage tourism products in the medium category use a limited permanent exhibition space reasonably well to try in some sense to contextualise their stories. The Lei Chung Uk Han Tomb Museum is one of very few publicly accessible examples of ancient built heritage (the Eastern Han Dynasty, c.AD 25–220) in Hong Kong and so provides important, tangible evidence of the long span of its material culture. Whilst the Ping Shan Tang Clan Museum is limited in its strictly historical contextualisation, it does at least attempt to put the evidence available into a social anthropological framework of this area of the New Territories. It comprises of three galleries: the Ping Shan Tang Clan Gallery that displays various relics belonging to the members of the Tang Clan who personally relate their history, customs and cultural life; the Gallery of Ping Shan Heritage Trail that introduces monuments and buildings along the Ping Shan Heritage Trail; and the Community Heritage Gallery which presents community-based special thematic exhibitions with a focus on the history and culture of the New Territories. This initiative has been seen as important to address international tourists, local Hong Kong visitors and indigenous inhabitants in terms of building a distinct identity (rather than a homogenised Hong Kong identity) for areas of the New Territories (Cheung, 2003). The Blue House has a more local community orientation and the University of Hong Kong promotes itself as being primarily a place of learning rather than a tourist attraction.

Only one-fifth of the revitalised heritage tourism products were regarded as attempting a highly extensive presentation of their story in relation to the wider Hong Kong story. The Hong Kong Heritage Discovery Centre, the former Whitfield Barracks at Kowloon Park, provides an overview of Hong Kong's archaeological material and built culture from earliest to recent times. It comprises two main sections – archaeological and built heritage. The former begins with a large chronological display of archaeological artefacts, and then focuses on discoveries from three main periods – prehistoric, and the Han and Ming dynasties. This evidence helps highlight Hong Kong's long-standing historical and cultural relationship with mainland China and Southeast Asia. A "Selected

Archaeological Finds" area allows visitors to browse findings excavated from across a wide range of locations and periods in Hong Kong. The Built Heritage section focuses on the connection between architecture and society, and features traditional Chinese, Western and modern styles. It traces the development of Hong Kong through the lens of built heritage, including the developments in conservation, revitalisation and cultural legacy.

Another significant contributor to building a picture of Hong Kong's story, albeit of more recent times, is the Dr Sun Yat-sen Museum. Occupying the revitalised Kom Tong Hall, formerly the residence of the local businessman Ho Kom-tong, the three permanent exhibitions tell the story of the building's conservation, Dr Sun Yat-sen and Modern China, and Hong Kong in Dr Sun Yat-sen's Time. This last gallery has particular relevance to the Hong Kong story as it highlights the key aspects, or "killer apps" as the historian Niall Ferguson (2011) might put it, of Hong Kong's political, social, cultural and economic scene which nurtured such an exceptional revolutionary leader and enabled him to learn new ideas, exchange information, operate relatively freely, recruit members, raise funds and transport supplies. Finally, both the Law Uk Folk Museum and Sam Tung Uk House Museum take a local history perspective (looking at Chai Wan and Tsuen Wan respectively) in their permanent exhibition galleries but make a significant effort to relate this to general socio-economic changes in Hong Kong.

Heritage tourism products in Hong Kong are managed by a wide range of organisations from private companies such as Cheung Kong (Holdings) Ltd and the Hong Kong and Shanghai Hotels Ltd to government departments (predominantly the Leisure and Cultural Services Department) and NGOs (such as the Hong Kong Heritage Conservation Foundation). They have also been developed as attractions over a number of decades and have a range of market positions, from hotel or shops to bespoke public attractions. They differ considerably in the scale in which the narrative is told – from a single graphic panel to entire permanent exhibitions. It may not be surprising, therefore, that there is very little consistency (in terms of narrative approach, key messages, communication techniques or aesthetic design values) between attractions managed by different organisations for different purposes. What is surprising is the almost total lack of consistency or coherence between products managed by the same organisation (notably the LCSD). There is no sense that these attractions help to collectively build a picture of Hong Kong's history through a deliberate and considered management of storytelling or design.

All of these attractions deal in some way with a historical narrative relating to Hong Kong, but there is no discernible historical framework that is consistently referred to. Reference is made to obvious milestones and timeframe divisions, such as dynastic periods, the ceding of Hong Kong to Britain in 1841, the Japanese occupation and the handover to China in 1997, but there is little sense of an overarching thematic narrative (particularly related to Hong Kong's colonial and post-colonial period) in which periods of time have been ascribed a socio-economic characteristic of development. Contrast this with the city-state of Singapore where even the smallest visitor centre loses no opportunity to reiterate a narrative of nation building with clear periods of development; so much so in fact that clients have privately confided to me that they feel that school children are starting to suffer from "timeline fatigue" and that the authorised version of Singapore's developmental progress is starting to become like wallpaper.

However, it is not as if Hong Kong is completely devoid of an officially sanctioned version of its own history. In as much as Hong Kong has an authorised history it is represented by the narrative presented in "The Story of Hong Kong" at the Museum of History. First established in 1975 and moved to its present site in Tsim Sha Tsui in 1998, this 7,000-square-metre permanent exhibition over eight galleries displays over 4,000 exhibits supported by 750 graphic panels, dioramas and multimedia programs in order to preserve and promote the historical and cultural heritage of Hong Kong. It covers a historical period from the Devonian Period (400 million years ago) and ends at the handover to China in 1997. It aims to "arouse the public interest in and introspection on the historical and cultural heritage of Hong Kong". In museum design terms, it uses the full range of interpretive display techniques available at its time of refit from simple graphics, traditional object cases and small-scale models to large-scale dioramas, walk-in reconstructions, and audio-visual shows. Its storyline "outlines the natural environment, folk culture and historical development of Hong Kong in a life-like manner" and very much emphasises the continuity of Hong Kong's history which stretches back for many hundreds of millions of years; so countering the Western textbook approach of tracing the development of the "barren rock" of the early nineteenth century to a modern metropolis transformed by trade and governance. The most prominent display of a historical personality is of Lin Zexu, a native of Fujian Province who operated in Guangdong, as the Chinese official tasked by the Qing Emperor Daoguang to stem the tide of the opium trade in China. The portraits of Hong Kong governors who, over the period of 150 years have arguably had the most impact on the socio-economic development of the city in recent times are consigned to a side corridor with little attempt to record their achievements. The overall impression is of a story of the Chinese inhabitants meeting and overcoming challenges in spite of (rather than because of) outside (i.e. foreign) colonial influences. The fact that such a significant effort of organising, managing and articulating Hong Kong's story has been almost completely ignored by the city's revitalised heritage products (even those also developed and run by the LCSD) is puzzling and surely a source of potential consistency and coherence across these storytelling vehicles.

Working in the field of museum and visitor attraction design since the early 1990s on projects in Hong Kong, I have seen the role of interpretive planning evolve. Interpretive planning is now a recognised and integral part of most public communication projects with a museum-like component issued by government departments. For example, this was the wording for a small exhibition gallery commissioned in 2009 by the Home Affairs Bureau for Civic Education Resource Centre in the Hong Kong Centre For Youth Development regarding the scope of works for the Interpretive Plan:

- Communication objectives
- Means of communication
- Visitor experience
- Exhibition walk through
- Visitor flow

However, unlike public museums, heritage buildings have in the last ten or so years been the subject of a government programme of relinquishing control to private developers, public-private partnerships or NGOs. The clearly discernible trend is that the further a heritage revitalisation project gets from government and the more it involves commercial entities, the less it strives to work a narrative into its adaptive re-use design, and by extension the less it incorporates interpretive planning into its processes. This has broken the link between an evolved, tried and tested project process promoted by the museum sector in Hong Kong and meant a more ad hoc and diverse approach to the development of such projects. One of the first major projects of heritage revitalisation in Hong Kong, and certainly one with the highest profile, was the adaptive re-use of the former Marine Police Headquarters in Tsim Sha Tsui.

The case of the adaptive re-use of the former Marine Police Headquarters

Located in Tsim Sha Tsui and built in 1884, this compound of buildings was declared a monument in 1994. In 2002, Hong Kong's parliament or Legislative Council (LegCo) agreed "to preserve, restore and convert the former Marine Police Headquarters (MPHQ) in Tsim Sha Tsui (the Project) for tourism related uses". The rationale for this was as follows:

There has been increasing public demand for more to be done to preserve our heritage assets. Given budgetary and other constraints on Government, there is a strong case for a new approach to preserve and exploit these facilities. One of the most suitable ways to do this is to engage private sector resources in suitable projects with commercial potential. This will help inject new ideas and a new dynamism into the process to convert our heritage assets to beneficial use. This will also enable Government to focus its resources on preservation work which does not offer a potential for private sector participation.

(LegCo File Ref: ESB CR 22/24/17)

The stated intention was to develop the site as a "heritage tourism facility". In May 2003, the Hong Kong Government awarded the tender for redevelopment to Flying Snow, a subsidiary of Cheung Kong (Holdings), on a 50-year land grant at HK$352.8 million. However, both during its development and after its opening in August 2009, the project was dogged by controversy. Conservationists' concerns included a large number of trees (149 of the original) lost and some century-old trees transplanted into

Figure 2.2 A temporary display in the forecourt of 1881 Heritage: the revitalisation of the former Marine Police Headquarters was criticised for obscuring heritage with over-commercialisation.

inadequate pots out of context with the original site, the loss of the topo-
graphy of Tsim Sha Tsui Hill and a failure to accurately measure the exact
floor size of the historic buildings (resulting in a 30% gain for the developer that was discovered after the handover and opening of the site).
More strikingly, the overall effect of the end result is one of a highly-
commercialised site, festooned with brand signage with little sense of the
original ambience of the site. Some experts in the field of conservation
such as Brian Anderson of the UK firm Purcell, Miller and Tritton believe
that the mistakes made are all part of a learning process: "It doesn't look
much like the Marine Police Headquarters anymore; you would be hard-
pressed to appreciate that – which is, arguably, its failing, (but) it certainly
is no worse that the early conservation projects in the UK." Other critics
are harsher. Referring to the architectural conservation of 1881, Professor
Lee Ho-yin, director of the architectural conservation programme at
University of Hong Kong says, "The worst that can be done to a heritage
building is to add an antique-looking pastiche to it."

The main interpretation in "1881 Heritage" takes the form of individual
elements of the site being described in terms of its architectural/historical
value by brass panels, but with little contextual information. It does have a
small dedicated exhibition gallery that contains a few desultory photographs
and models but, as mentioned, this is primarily used to promote the developer Cheung Kong's role in the revitalisation of the site through a video
presentation.

It is striking how little time or space is devoted to telling the story of the
site. Interpretation was clearly given the merest cursory consideration in the
adaptive re-use of this very significant building for Hong Kong's heritage.
How such an important public asset in Hong Kong can be revitalised as a
heritage tourism attraction and yet communicate so little of worth for public
education is a major concern. What happens in the process of development
to diminish or sideline the role of interpretation in such projects and what
can be done about it? From a political point of view, there may not have
been the expertise within the government project team confident to deal with
a prominent heritage revitalisation site of such complexity. This would have
led to the conclusion that the most expedient way forward would be to take a
developer-led approach instead of involving conservation specialists to set
the fundamental parameters and direction from an early stage in the project.
Given the political and media climate at the time, the government may have
felt it could deflect or escape any potential criticism for any perceived fail-
ings in the project in this way. Or it may genuinely have felt that the required
expertise lay best within the property development sector. However, setting
the project up in this way meant that it was fundamentally skewed in a direction that emphasised commercial considerations over conservation concerns

from the beginning, resulting in the emphasis of pastiche architectural solutions, poor conservation practice, destruction of historic fabric and understanding, and a branded ephemeral image over heritage authenticity.

What is going on with heritage revitalisation projects in Hong Kong?

Maxwell (2005) states that experiential knowledge is one of four main sources from which to construct a conceptual framework for study (the others being existing theory and research, pilot and exploratory research, and thought experiments). Due to the lack of both extensive literature and exploratory research on the role of interpretation in adaptive re-use urban heritage revitalisation projects, the research approach primarily relied on my experiential knowledge as an industry "insider" and an ongoing iterative thought framework to model what seem to be the issues (Figure 2.3).

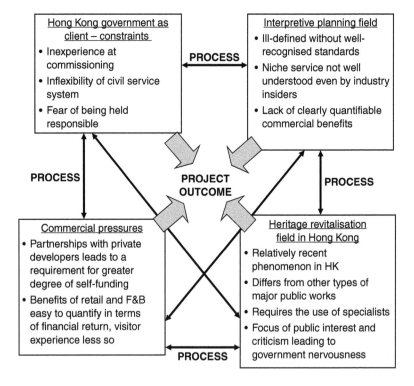

Figure 2.3 Concept map of "What I think is going on" with regard to the interpretive role in heritage revitalisation projects in Hong Kong.

The inclusion of a meaningful interpretive experience for visitors in the project outcome of adapting a heritage building for re-use seems to be affected by four main factors – the constraints of the Hong Kong government as client, the interpretive planning field itself, the nature of the heritage revitalisation field in Hong Kong and commercial pressures on the eventual product.

Hong Kong government as client – constraints

Inexperience in commissioning: the nature of the Hong Kong civil service is that staff move on a relatively regular basis. Officers may be moved from department to department every few years. Commissioning large-scale capital spend projects might happen only once in a particular officer's career and, given that these projects often take several years from beginning to end, they might not see any given project through to completion. Even in the case of the Architectural Services Department, large-scale projects in the museum or visitor attraction field are few and far between. This leads to a leakage of institutional memory about how to successfully prosecute such projects and a tendency to reinvent the wheel when each new project comes along.

Inflexibility of the civil service system: by its very nature government civil services tend to be slow at adopting new practices or keeping up with industry trends. There tends to be a time lag in recognising or adopting ideas that might be evolving relatively fast in the more adaptable and dynamic commercial world. Added to this is the difficulty of seconding talent (e.g. personnel who may have experience of large scale capital project works with a public communications/tourism outcome) to projects where their experience might be maximised.

Fear of being held responsible: the post-1997 Hong Kong government has been subject to an unprecedented level of public and media scrutiny which seems to have led to a certain level of nervousness within the civil service of being held responsible for large cultural capital projects (outside of infrastructure). This is exemplified by the slow progress on the West Kowloon Cultural District (originally suggested in 1998 and still ongoing) and the initial approach of giving the entire project over to a single developer, from which the Hong Kong government retreated in 2005. Whilst the idea of partnering with developers to revitalise heritage assets could be seen as a laudable attempt to bring fresh, more commercial approaches to the process, it could also be seen as a halfway house between pushing responsibility wholly onto developers and the government taking full responsibility for such projects.

Interpretive planning field

Ill-defined without well-recognised standards: as we have seen, this is a professional field that has been evolving only since the 1980s and does not have clear, standards for either its process or delivery.

Niche service not well understood even by industry insiders: this is a very specialised service that even some of the largest design/fabrication companies involved in the business of visitor attraction design are not intimately familiar with.

Lack of clearly quantifiable commercial benefits: unlike other creative consultancies that might be involved in a heritage revitalisation project (such as architectural or retail interior design) it is hard to quantify the financial benefit to the project of telling a meaningful story.

Heritage revitalisation field in Hong Kong

Relatively recent phenomenon in Hong Kong: as we have seen this recent growth in interest about Hong Kong identity has renewed calls for heritage assets to be preserved and made useful to the wider public through adaptive re-use. However, this is a relatively recent phenomenon which means that Hong Kong is on a steep learning curve to learn the lessons of best practice in this field.

Differs from other types of major public works: the specialist nature of this type of project – involving a wide range of consultancies (from engineers to experiential designers) in a complex process – means that the standard government procurement template or processes are hard to simply apply directly.

Requires the use of specialists: the appointment and management of a wide range of interdependent specialists (from conservation architects to multimedia producers) is a major challenge of tendering and project management coordination.

Focus of public interest and criticism leading to government nervousness: the passions raised since the demolition of the Star Ferry Terminal in 2007 have meant a keen public and press interest in perceived government inaction/incompetence/collusion with developers over the redevelopment of heritage sites. Added to this is the growing realisation of the link between heritage sites, collective memory and Hong Kong identity that has heightened sensitivities around this type of project.

Commercial pressures

Partnerships with private developers lead to a requirement for greater degree of self-funding: a major reason for government to involve private enterprises is to minimise public money needed to support the new entity going forward. This means that a strong commercial imperative for the heritage tourism product to be financially independent is introduced, leading in turn to commercial pressures becoming a major deciding factor in the process of development.

Benefits of retail and F&B easy to quantify in terms of financial return, visitor experience less so: the need for income means that the benefit of incorporating and maximising the floor space given over the rent-paying retailers and restaurants is self-evident. It is harder to quantify the benefit to the project of turning over space to historical interpretation (for which it may not be possible to charge a fee) other than a sense of public duty.

Research issues

The revitalisation of heritage sites is becoming the primary vehicle by which heritage assets are brought into the public visitation domain in Hong Kong. This process is inextricably linked with the heritage tourism experience; so this study took a combined, adapted model as a framework to examine and interrogate the results of the intended methodology. This combined Timothy and Boyd's (2003) model of heritage tourism experience with McKercher and du Cros' (2002) tourism framework in order to give a more complete context within which to examine the role of interpretive planning in heritage revitalisation projects in Hong Kong (Figure 2.4).

With reference to this model, the study tested the specific question:

> Why – when the stated primary intention of so many urban heritage revitalisation projects is to tell the story of the site for the purposes of cultural tourism – does the interpretive element of these projects so often get diminished during the course of implementation and what can be done about it?

It is posited that this can be visualised in the following way (Figure 2.5).

The intention was to define the factors that may be acting as a depressing influence on the end outcome of perceived representation of the story in heritage revitalisation projects in Hong Kong and discover ways in which positive steps might be taken to raise the end perception of the representation of the site's story closer to the initial perceived importance.

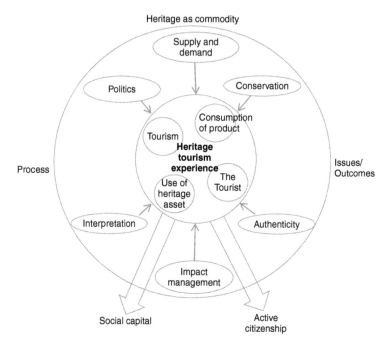

Figure 2.4 Adapted Timothy and Boyd's model of heritage tourism experience with McKercher and Du Cros' tourism framework.

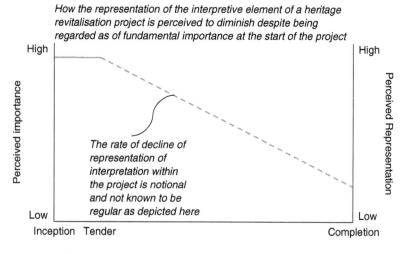

Figure 2.5 How the representation of the interpretive element of a heritage revitalisation project is perceived to diminish.

Methods of collecting data

Semi-structured interviews were used. Given the specialist nature of the topic, the sample size was necessarily small and the criteria for selection deliberately focused on interviewees with prior and specialist knowledge of the adaptive re-use heritage field in Hong Kong. In-depth interviews were conducted in a setting that the interviewee found comfortable to express their own views. This was either in their own place of work or in an informal social setting. Interview questions were developed creatively in order to engage the interest of the subject, relate to issues of relevance to them and stimulate debate about topical heritage and revitalisation projects in Hong Kong, or comparable international examples.

The study did not relate to a single project but rather the phenomenon of how interpretation is used in the heritage revitalisation sector in Hong Kong. The expectation was that the goal and purpose of the case study would enable transferability (Lincoln and Guba, 2000) of conclusions drawn to future projects in the sector. It was expected that each practitioner would be likely to go off on a tangent that is most relevant to their discipline. Indeed, it was regarded as desirable that the interviewee be allowed some latitude to talk about relevant issues or examples that they feel strongly about, whilst always being brought back to the main focus of the interview. Therefore, the study had a basic structure that covered some key issues related to heritage and conservation within a semi-structured approach. Interview questions included:

- What are your views on the Hong Kong government approach to heritage revitalisation projects in Hong Kong?
- What is your experience of the way that interpretation works within projects for the adaptive re-use of heritage buildings in Hong Kong or elsewhere?
- What are the commercial pressures on such projects and how do you think these affect the outcome?
- Is there a more strategic role for interpretation to play in these projects?
- If so, what form would this take?

Interviews were conducted in English and typically lasted between one and two hours; they were recorded and subsequently transcribed. It was soon clear that the role of interpretation meant different things to different people and that the different perspectives of the interviewees provided a wide range of responses. Flexibility was allowed for as the study progressed in order to be able to accommodate findings "grounded" in the ongoing data collection and analysis (Maxwell 2005). The discussions were exploratory and often wide-ranging so a combination of case study (heritage revitalisation projects in Hong Kong) and grounded theory approach was taken to analyse the data, allowing the data itself to reveal aspects of the phenomenon and create its own framework with minimal pre-conceived ideas.

Sample selection

A purposeful sample, necessarily limited by professional experience, of architects, a specialist designer, academic and high-ranking civil servant from the heritage and conservation sector in Hong Kong was selected. This spread of interviewees ensured that the range of specialists, heritage revitalisation project stakeholders and commissioners from both public and private sectors were represented. The interviewees were as follows:

Interviewee 1 (I1): a senior member of the Antiquities Advisory Board (AAB). The AAB is a statutory body established under the Antiquities and Monuments Ordinance (Cap. 53) to advise the Antiquities Authority on any matters relating to antiquities and monuments. It comprises 23 members (including the Chairman), who are all appointed in their personal capacity.

Interviewee 2 (I2): a distinguished academic in the field of heritage conservation who teaches interpretation of heritage sites as well as being an UNESCO/ICOMOS World Heritage Evaluator.

Interviewee 3 (I3): a founding member of a leading specialist architectural company who has been involved in numerous cultural and heritage revitalisation projects over more than 30 years in both Hong Kong and China.

Interviewee 4 (I4): a Partner in a company with over 70 years' experience in conservation architecture and urban design in the evaluation of town centre developments.

Interviewee 5 (I5): a Director with an international experiential design consultancy with over 30 years' experience working across 50 countries working for government, corporate and institutional clients on projects ranging from large-scale masterplans and strategic feasibility studies to design and build projects; large-scale museum, heritage, eco-park, zoo, exhibition and interior designs.

Data analysis

As the primary form of data was interview transcripts, the data analysis used a wide range of text analysis techniques including reading and re-reading of interviews, transcribing, coding, categorisation by theme and issue using organisational, substantive and theoretical categories.

Other than the general attributes such as gender, class and age that I brought into the research project, the factors that are particularly relevant to my positionality in relation to this topic include my education, professional background and experience, family history and political outlook and beliefs. It is reasonable to assume that my experience was a major source of insights, hypotheses and validity checks within the research, especially as there are few well-developed theories to apply or explicit strategies to harness in this research.

Limitations of the study

The restricted nature of the sample is both a limitation and indicative of the state of interpretive planning in Hong Kong. As mentioned, by its very nature heritage revitalisation is a relatively new phenomenon in Hong Kong, and, being in its early days, the Hong Kong government has tended to draw on expertise from outside or with knowledge of the field outside of Hong Kong. This has meant that, in order to get the views of relevant experts in the field, it has been necessary to be highly selective resulting in a small sample that is also dominated by non-Hong Kong Chinese interviewees. As such, the views expressed cannot be regarded as comprehensive but can be seen as an insightful snapshot of the current status of interpretive planning in heritage revitalisation projects in Hong Kong. It should also be noted that all respondents have long associations (some over 30 years) with the Hong Kong heritage scene with relevant professional or academic experience of the topic under discussion.

References

Brokensha, P. and Guldberg, H. (1992). *Cultural tourism in Australia: a report on cultural tourism*, Canberra: AGPS.

Cheung, C.H. Sidney (1999). "The meanings of a heritage trail in Hong Kong". *Annals of Tourism Research* 26(3): 570–588.

Cheung, S. (2003). "Remembering through space: the politics of heritage in Hong Kong". *International Journal of Heritage Studies* 9(1): 7–26.

Cheung, S. (2008). "Wetland tourism in Hong Kong: from birdwatcher to mass Ecotourist". In *Asian tourism: growth and change*, by Cochrane, J. Oxford; Amsterdam: Elsevier.

Ferguson, N. (2011). *Civilization: the west and the rest*, London; New York: Allen Lane.

Henderson, J. (2001). "Heritage, identity and tourism in Hong Kong". *International Journal of Heritage Studies*, 7(3): 219–235.

HKGIS (1963–2010). *Hong Kong Yearbook*. Hong Kong: Government Information Services.

Ho, P. and McKercher, B. (2008). "Managing heritage resources as tourism products". In *Cultural and heritage tourism in Asia and the Pacific*, edited by Prideaux, B., Timothy, D. and Chon, K. London: Routledge.

Konrad, V. (1982). "Historical artifacts as recreational resources". In *Recreational land use, perspectives on its evolution in Canada* edited by Walsh, G. and Marsh, J., Ottawa: Carleton University Press.

Leung, K. and Wong, Y. (1994). *25 years of social development in Hong Kong*, Hong Kong: The University of Hong Kong.

Lincoln, Y. and Guba, E. (2000). "The only generalization is: there is no generalization". In *Case study method: key issues, key texts*, edited by Gomm, R., Hammersley, M. and Foster, P. London: SAGE.

Maxwell, J.A. (2005). *Qualitative research design: an interactive approach*. Thousand Oaks, CA: Sage Publications.

McKercher, B. (2002). "Towards a classification of cultural tourists". *International Journal of Tourism Research* 4, 29–38.

McKercher, B., Ho, P., du Cros, H. and Chow, B. (2002). "Actvities-based segmentation of the cultural tourism market". *Journal of Travel and Tourism Marketing* 12(1): 23–46.

3   Findings and discussion

The responses of the interviewees to the questions were analysed and categorised. Evidence of saturation was found in the universal confirmation that there is indeed a problem with the interpretive outcome of heritage revitalisation projects in Hong Kong and to some extent the diagnosis of the causes for this phenomenon. There were divergent opinions on how these problems might be addressed consistent with the different professional backgrounds and perspectives of the respondents.

The most frequently recurring and common propositions were as follows:

1   There are very few good examples of interpretation in heritage revitalisation projects in Hong Kong
2   There are definable reasons why telling the story of these sites gets lost in the end result of such projects
3   The way projects have been and are structured has an impact on the quality of interpretation
4   There are steps the Hong Kong government should take to promote interpretation within heritage revitalisation projects
5   Hong Kong society is changing and this will have implications for interpretation in the future

Few good examples of interpretation in heritage revitalisation projects in Hong Kong

All the respondents expressed the view that there are very few examples of good interpretation or storytelling in heritage revitalisation projects to date in Hong Kong. A typical statement was:

> I can't think of any really good examples of heritage development, redevelopment or heritage re-use in Hong Kong to be frank.

The level of conservation of the buildings themselves was regarded as equivalent to where the UK was in the 1960s and 70s. However, it is seen as a fast-developing field due to renewed public and government focus. The understanding displayed of interpretation and storytelling in such projects was variously described as "basic", "not high" and not of an international standard. Moreover, what stories are being told, why and to whom are all seen to be problematic:

> If you were to just ask me, in general, about revitalisation and interpretation and storytelling, the storytelling wouldn't come out high from my point of view.... I've never been convinced about what stories are being told and why and to whom and all that kind of thing.
>
> (I2)

There was a general difficulty in recalling any significant number of examples but two projects were mentioned consistently as examples of how not to do it (1881 Heritage) and as a good example (Tai O Police Station). 1881 Heritage was seen as over-commercialised, poor conservation due to the destruction of key, unique aspects of the site that would allow visitors to make sense of its historical context and trying to make the building appear pristine, as well as an absence of meaningful interpretation or storytelling:

> 1881 Heritage is a recent example and it's had a pretty bad press, hasn't it? But I think for me the biggest concern is about all what they did to the context, which was completely destroyed as I understand it. It was on the brow of a hill, which was thickly wooded; that's all gone. We've now got a rather banal shopping – open air shopping mall in its place. So, as a visitor experience, it is exclusive and it's overtly commercial and underneath all the glitz, there is a historical building there somewhere. So, I think that's a lost opportunity.
>
> (I4)

> [1881 is] a bloody awful example really. I think what they did with the landscaping was atrocious, essentially re-levelled it making it more accessible to shoppers. They essentially destroyed the nature of the site which was an observatory in a prominent location at the end of Tsim Sha Shui. There's little to no interpretation within that.
>
> (I5)

The revitalisation of the Aberdeen/Ap Lei Chau Waterfront was also highlighted as a particular offender with the lack of any effort to contextualise the sites through storytelling seen as a key oversight on the part of the Hong Kong government's role:

> There's no narrative, there's no access to the information. You can't scratch the surface. It's just a photo and a label and that's it. No information of any sort whatsoever. And the opportunity there for an interpretive experience is enormous – I mean really enormous.... It's such a lost opportunity because it's so thin. There's just nothing really that you'd really want to go back and have another look. It's just a random collection of photographs, badly labelled, very uninformative in terms of just the written information about each image. And it's done in a way which is honestly "school-boy." This is something which I think is a massive lost opportunity and we see it repeated again and again.
>
> (I3)

The adaptation of Wedding Card St (Lee Tung St) in Wanchai opened in November 2015 was regarded as an example of creating fake heritage rather than trying to re-use heritage buildings in situ and interpret them:

> Another bad example is Wedding Card Street which is entirely demolished and it's still under redevelopment. You've got fake heritage being built in that area with really horrible mouldings that are meant to look old and the life of that street has gone forever now, totally lost.
>
> (I5)

However, the adaptive re-use of the former Tai O Police was seen as more successful, as witnessed by the receipt of a UNESCO award for its revitalisation but was also regarded as being successful in a Hong Kong context rather than to an international standard. It was seen as being strong in the work it had done with the involvement of the local community:

> If I'm using international standards, I must humbly say there are very, very few – if any – very successful cases in Hong Kong that could relay the history and story behind any historic building or developments to the general public or to the visitors. The key issue here facing Hong Kong is, in general, the heritage conservation is still a relatively new subject to the community as a whole.... Of course, by Hong Kong standards, there are! There are a few like the Old Tai O Police Station, the regular police station is now converted to a Heritage hotel, a boutique hotel. But in the police station case, they've actually developed a kind of soft approach by inviting, well actually tapping

into those policemen who have worked in the station in the past. Also, the local people who have actually interacted with those who have worked in the station and interacted with the station in all kinds of ways.

(I1)

Indeed, adaptive re-use was seen as becoming more successful in other recent projects whilst the interpretive elements were still lagging behind:

PMQ you could argue is a reasonably successful adaptive re-use. Although I doubt that many people that go there have any understanding of what the building was originally used for or what the site was used for before that. From the interpretive point of view, it's not great but from the adaptive re-use point of view it is a reasonable space considering the constraints that they've got.

(I5)

It was generally agreed that opportunities have been and are being lost to interpret heritage revitalisation sites well:

I think the territory is littered with these kinds of lost opportunities, honestly. Murray House was another story, I mean where's the story of it? What is it? Is it really just a kind of Disney-esque shopping venue? Really? Isn't there something attached to that which is of value?

(I3)

The general feeling among respondents, therefore, is not only are there few examples of good interpretation in Hong Kong but that many of them are examples of how not to carry out these sorts of projects. The integration of interpretive elements that tell the stories of these sites seems to be lagging behind the adaptive re-use of the buildings themselves. The next category of proposition derived from the interview responses was an attempt to shed light on why this might be.

Definable reasons why the story gets lost in the end result of such projects

The analysis of why the interpretation of historical content or storytelling gets lost in these projects, even when it may have been an important reason justifying public money being spent on it in the first place, focused primarily on the role of the Hong Kong government in commissioning and managing the projects. Some cynicism was expressed as to whether the stated intention of such projects was genuinely held by the commissioners of the project:

> In terms of heritage projects, I'm not sure the real remit for them is ever to interpret the story or preserve the history of the site. Really, it is a political issue where they are trying to retain the building on the site and adaptively reuse it. And from that comes all the other issues of adaptive reuse. The element of interpretation and the storyline and the history of the project is usually a tack-on and it's something that has to be done that needs to be seen to have been done.
>
> (I5)

This feeling was compounded by a sense that the impetus to start to look at the interpretive aspect of these projects has come largely from the public and the government has been reactive rather than proactive in it:

> I don't really think the government is doing anything to construct the environment, as such. What I'm saying is that, the government in the past ten, 15 years has been kind of responding to certain calls from the general public.
>
> (I1)

However, the lack of experience in government in dealing with such complex and sensitive projects was seen as a problem at a fundamental level:

> The tendency within government to often try and take control over revitalisation efforts, applying their own – to be very blunt – lack of expertise to resolving problems that do need sensitivity and expertise, is a bit distressing.
>
> (I3)

Once a project is initiated, it was also felt that there seems to be a lack of engagement with the subject matter in question by civil service project managers and, by extension, a perceived or assumed lack of interest amongst the Hong Kong public. This was deemed to be particularly true at the middle management level of government project administration:

> When it actually drops down through the lower echelons of that structure, within that organization, it gets lost.... I mean the engagement with the subject matter just gets very weak. They're just not bloody interested!
>
> (I3)

This has translated into a greater degree of focus on the hardware of conservation projects rather than the software; an emphasising of the tangible over the intangible, building over story:

> The general concern of the community on conservation is, again, rather on the hardware side more than on the software side because people know very, very little about the history of Hong Kong.
>
> (I1)

A possible explanation for this perceived lack of interest in Hong Kong's story was the way local history was taught in the education curriculum under British colonial rule:

> I think the colonial government contributed a huge lot to that kind of context because they don't want people to talk about history. So, it's not hidden as such, but there's no general effort to push these ideas as a whole, which will then lead to pain, unhappiness and all kinds of things.
>
> (I1)

Contentious issues such as the Opium War, and the role of some of the founding British companies of Hong Kong in it, and the fact that, far from being a "barren rock" or a humble fishing village before 1842, Hong Kong had been part of the flourishing "Silk Road of the Sea" (as proven by recent archaeological findings of Tang Dynasty ships) were simply brushed under the carpet:

> Both governments really don't want to talk about that part of history. They don't want us to talk about, "Oh, why was there an Opium War and how does that relate to the main businesses in Hong Kong?" In Hong Kong, the big British names like Jardine, you know, Hutchison – for most, it's just a name.
>
> (I1)

For instance, the resistance by the population of the New Territories to the imposition of colonial rule following the leasing to Britain of this area in 1898 is still not widely understood by people in Hong Kong. This allowed pre-1842 history to be simply disregarded by the colonial education system and any sense of indigenous identity expunged. On top of this was layered the fact that up until 1950, there had been a very permeable border, allowing people and goods to move back and forth relatively freely, but with the start of the Cold War and the forming of the People's Republic of China in

1949 this freedom of movement had ended. These events brought a new influx of migrants. Many of those with capital to establish what later became well-known companies in fact had no link to Hong Kong and were from the Yangtse Delta – Shanghai, Suzhou, Zhejiang and so on. Without a sense of attachment or ancestral ties to Hong Kong, this influential section of Chinese society had no incentive to see the place as anything more than a transitory place:

> The general historical context of Hong Kong has been buried, in a way, from a social development point of view. It's because of our very unique colonial history and change of sovereignty.
>
> (I1)

This is seen as explaining much of the apparent apathy amongst even civil servants running heritage-related projects and the emergence of a new interest amongst the younger generation. It is only with the post-80s generation that Hong Kong people are really getting a sense of permanent identity and nostalgia about the history of their own city. But this also means that without a firm foundation of agreed history, the reawakening of interest can spur a range of contesting versions:

> If you don't try to kind of build something in the education system, somehow the facts and the truth will be lost through time. And then when people try to kind of pick them back up again, by researching and that kind of thing, they're subject to very different interpretations. And that's exactly what's happening now.
>
> (I1)

Far from seeing interpretation as a way of ensuring that the narrative element of a revitalisation project is dealt with to a high standard, there has been a tendency to view the process of storytelling within projects with a certain amount of suspicion:

> Where you have a situation where you need somebody to take a certain level of risk to make a statement, to be maybe even controversial, you're dealing with the wrong authority then because their inherent and natural position would be: no risks.
>
> (I3)

So, not only is there a perceived lack of interest but there is also a sense that there is an inherent threat within the contested story of Hong Kong that makes the interpreting of it fraught with difficulties and full of pitfalls.

Added to this is a seemingly greater sensitiveness to criticism within government since the handover compared to other places:

> I know the government is very sensitive to public opinion here in a much greater way than is the case in the UK, so I can understand why government is troubled by this, as well as other things. Therefore, its default position is always to look for the way of avoiding issues rather than meeting them. Because that's part of the culture of Hong Kong, it rather mitigates against taking initiatives.
>
> (I4)

This lack of engagement with the content and nervousness about how to deal with it may well be due to the early stage of development of revitalisation heritage projects and developing expertise within the field of interpretation in Hong Kong:

> There's no standard practice. It's only after, case after case, Hong Kong starts to kind of make it more rich. And we're grooming the right people and now we have more people kind of knowing what they would like to do and knowing what they have to do to make it right. Whether they can do a good job is a separate issue. At least, I think, we have an understanding of what good practice is all about. So, I think we're at that stage.
>
> (I1)

To be fair to the Hong Kong government, it is not as though the local design industry is regarded as being brimming with expertise or desire to deal with the interpretive elements of projects either:

> When you are engaging with companies, creative services companies, the minute you take them out of the norm into a slightly unknown area like interpretive experience, they'd be completely lost, they wouldn't know how to think about it. I mean who wants to take the responsibility for being challenged at the end of the day? Because at the end of the day, anything to do with heritage means you're actually writing something about history.
>
> (I3)

However, the nervousness in government (as the main commissioning body of heritage revitalisation projects) about engaging and defining the Hong Kong story has meant that an agreed narrative across a range of projects has not been prominent:

There's not an authorized version [of Hong Kong's history], unless what we can see as an authorized version through the Hong Kong History Museum, that's as close as we come.

(I2)

The result of these factors has fed into the way that projects have been structured, tendered and managed by governments to date, leading to the unsatisfactory outcomes discussed.

Project structure has an impact on the quality of interpretation

Government departments that are averse to risk either from a public relations point of view or project management perspective find it difficult to build into a formal, quantifiable tender process a task that it not well understood in the local design industry or that requires flexibility in terms of the project timeline and outcomes:

The conservation management plan tends to be, increasingly for many, a mechanical exercise. That is not why you have a conservation management plan! You have one so you can be a good manager of a resource that matters to a community. It's that simple! So, it's the same with interpretation. We're always giving places meaning and that meaning we give today, will be different in five years, just because we're different. So, we introduced a fair amount of relativity to the discussion and with interpretation it's exactly the same thing. You know, no story is fixed in time, fixed in space.

(I2)

This makes interpretation a difficult element to manage and inevitably leads to compromise of those elements of the project that are seen as problematic or a luxury (i.e. those whose value is hard to quantify) at the final or implementation stages of the project:

There are always financial constraints in everything that you do, that goes without saying. That's reality. But the financial constraints are quite severe, I think, at the backend, at the implementation. An awful lot of compromise is indulged in at that level, which is unfortunate.

(I3)

This is particularly true where revitalisation projects are being conducted with an aim of income generation to support operational costs, meaning that interpretation is judged on those terms rather than on its contribution to the aims or mission of the project as a whole:

> There is no body that is recognized as an authority who can adjudicate on the worthiness of what you produce. And therefore, I guess it's going to be seen as a commodity that costs money.
>
> (I4)

There is a divergence between interviewees as to how the interpretive element should be built into the structure of the project. Consultants prefer to see some form of formal recognition of its role within the setup of the project with the government engaging more directly with the content, especially at the brief creation stage:

> I think also there is perhaps a tendency to abdicate that responsibility because it's in the "too hard to do" box. Well, that I think is a major problem. I think it's a big, big, big mistake to allow that abdication to happen. Because what it means then is that you go out, you engage your consultants to come in and do all this whizzy stuff, to write the stories and do all of that stuff for you. But because you haven't actually done any thinking about it fundamentally yourself, you're confronted with something that is almost impossible to understand.
>
> (I3)

It was thought by one consultant that organisations such as the AMO set elements of the brief that touch on content to be interpreted without actually stipulating how the story should be told:

> AMO tend to set very dry criteria for things. So, they'll come in and they'll designate protection of certain heritage elements and that then gets tacked on to a project as a requirement. Nobody's dealing with it in a way, almost like an adaptive reuse of the heritage story in a way to be able to think about how best to communicate that narrative from AMO's very analytical approach of "this is heritage" into something that could be translated into something usable and relevant for people. There's no one doing that so it's a requirement on the job but nobody really knows how to take it forward and make it work in synergy with the actual overall development itself.
>
> (I5)

In other words, heritage is incorporated into government-led projects as a static element without a sense of how to communicate it or of its value to the wider community; it is seen as a requirement rather than a resource. Given that this approach does not seem to have produced notable examples of interpretation within revitalised heritage projects to date, the question remains what steps should the Hong Kong government take to promote interpretation within these projects?

Steps to promote interpretation within heritage revitalisation projects

There were a number of steps that the interviewees identified that the government could take to improve the efficacy and representation of interpretive storytelling in the end result of heritage revitalisation projects: (i) capacity building (ii) creating the right market environment (iii) resolving where the responsibility should lie in government (iv) creating incentives (v) establishing an independent body to oversee issues of historical narrative for Hong Kong.

Capacity building

There was some divergence between the private and public sector interviewees. The former saw the need to improve performance and build capacity at the senior level of civil service management to enable project leaders to be confident and capable of dealing and engaging with interpretation and narrative. This in turn, it was believed, would filter down through the hierarchy rather than the current situation where middle managers were unwilling to deal with controversial subject matter because they knew they would get no support or input from above:

> There needs to be that kind of storytelling capability within whatever the group is or department or division or area of ownership, if you like, within government.... At the stage of formation of the brief, there needs to be a lot more creative thinking. That means, within government itself.... I think it's at the policy level – the level at which you decide that we need to do this project – that's where it needs to be. So why? What's the point? What's the purpose? What are we trying to do? What are we trying to achieve? What is the story that we're trying to explore?
>
> (I3)

It was acknowledged that by the nature of the way the civil service works, even when such secondary expertise is built up in a particular department (such as the Architectural Services Department), often personnel get moved on and the knowledge base is lost as it is not regarded as a core expertise. However, this could be done by either bringing interpretive expertise into the government for projects or specific training.

The public sector saw capacity building more along the lines of maintaining data sources to enable agencies or individuals outside of government to engage in interpretive activities that could contribute to the heritage revitalisation field:

> You need to have the information pool which can be shared; commonly shared to everybody. We're not there, we're far from there. But now, individuals may join into picking bits and pieces and try to kind of create their own story.
>
> (I1)

In line with this more laissez-faire approach preferred by the government, the example of Hong Kong's free market economy was seen to be a successful model to bring new expertise into heritage revitalisation within a context set by government:

> That takes a good deal of effort from different professions including the government to create the environment, including – when I say the environment, I mean including they need the market, to set the right agenda, to nurture the appropriate human resources and then using, kind of responding to the growing awareness of the community as a whole. To create the right environment to raise public concerns and awareness of heritage conservation.
>
> (I1)

Rather than government investing in and bringing in expertise itself, the setting of the business agenda, creating the opportunities and issuing the right sort of tenders in order to encourage growth in the private sector that would actually be doing the heritage revitalisation work was seen as important:

> I'm sure they would have to kind of engage a proper interpreter to develop a new story and that's happening … there are commercial organizations, there are NGOs working on in this particular field and it's developing now. So that goes back to what I said earlier on: it's the government, through different means, as long as they create the right market environment.
>
> (I1)

There is a sense that non-professionals are somehow better placed to research stories about Hong Kong's history:

> There are many things for the general public that we can do. Because there are actually a lot of things which you cannot find in the system. Even if you're a professional historian, I've seen so many. They're always, always a lot of kind of human or social network kind of stories that you cannot possibly dig up from formal documents. So, I think that's the key area that I would like to see being developed in the future.... I think the government should only try and enrich that and allow the professional or amateur interpreters to kind of redefine the right ingredients in that pool to work out their own version for particular projects or just for education or leisure purpose.
>
> (I1)

This is seen as being in the tradition of how the Hong Kong government has always encouraged entrepreneurship through competition in the marketplace. And it would be fair to say that this is often at the request or lobbying by the market players themselves to be "left alone" (particularly in the case of Hong Kong's most successful private sector, the financial industries). However, the professionals currently in the marketplace seem to be asking for more government engagement in their role as guardians of Hong Kong cultural assets. Moreover, the government's encouragement of "amateur" participants to enter the market by forming NGOs or not-for-profit organisations is likely to promote interest amongst a small, elite group of participants who can afford to participate on a charitable basis.

Creating the right market environment

Those with a more government perspective prefer to create a more informal arrangement with amateur and/or non-profit organisations getting more involved:

> I don't really think that the government should be encouraged to kind of build something very rigid on a contractual basis. But rather, I think, I'm still rather more keen to see the government provide adequate incentive and soft infrastructure to encourage the general development or awareness of the history of Hong Kong; in association with built heritage or archaeological conservation.
>
> (I1)

However, again some specialists in the field felt this may be a way of government absolving themselves of responsibility:

> By passing it onto NGOs, they get to absolve themselves from any particular issues. Especially with NGOs because they're considered "good" – good entities doing things for the wellbeing of the society. So, it's a way out for them on that issue.
>
> (I5)

The government seems to be more comfortable focusing on the hardware whilst letting the software of the storytelling reside outside the boundaries of even the project team:

> The key issue, as I said, is that we could not be using the same set of criteria because on the hardware side, it's something you can see and touch. It's very obvious. But the history side is so different. You don't really know how deep you can dig. The government doesn't really know what's out there. Better not for the government or anybody or institution to define the boundary for us. You better leave it to the project proponent to find out as much as possible. And the assessors to kind of make the best judgment on it.
>
> (I1)

This certainly seems to bear out the perception amongst the professional consultants involved in such projects that the Hong Kong government believes that the historical narrative should not be within the purview of the core government team but of the outside project proponent, with the government acting as an arbiter of what is acceptable. However, perhaps this is actually an acknowledgement of a need to learn from outside by those within government circles:

> Why is Hong Kong the most praised free economy in the world? We look at a lot of private sector projects. They know they have to do the value add to get a project right. Where do they learn it from? They can learn it from overseas, they can learn it from competitors in Hong Kong. And they know they have to do something if they want to be better than other people.
>
> (I1)

The government view is that it should devise a way to set criteria for narrative provision within the project but not be prescriptive about the details of that content and allow free market forces to hone the quality of the content provision within these projects.

Resolving where the responsibility should lie in government

Participants reported that the current situation means that a heritage project may fall within the remit of at least half a dozen government departments. There may not be sufficient knowledge or expertise related to heritage revitalisation process or policy within any one department to confidently move the project forward and given the notoriously "silo" mentality of government (which is by no means solely a Hong Kong problem) it is difficult to create coherent and coordinated outcomes:

> I think the government lacks any particular entity that is managing any of those things. And I think the government lacks any entity that's managing creative, cultural development at all. There's nobody doing it and it's left to individual departments to manage individual projects and areas. There's no expertise developed to come up with a plan for things. And that's a major issue.

(I5)

For instance, the Antiquities Advisory Board (AAB), which is the statutory body set up to advise the Antiquities Authority on any matters relating to antiquities and monuments, comes under the Development Bureau. Over the past decade or so this has made sense as a lot of issues associated with the conservation of heritage buildings have been simply about ensuring that they are not earmarked for redevelopment and pulled down. This required the various departments under the Development Bureau – the Lands, Planning and Buildings Departments – to work together. However, fundamentally the Development Bureau does not (nor has it been set up to have) a cultural dimension. This means that the projects with an explicitly cultural mission have been initiated and progressed by areas of the government without the relevant expertise or remit.

The department under whose jurisdiction culture does come is the Leisure and Cultural Services Department (LCSD). This department's remit covers the management of sporting and performing arts venues, meaning that its civil servants do not necessarily have experience in administering conservation, cultural tourism or heritage projects specifically. It was felt that the role of overseeing heritage-related projects should be given a more prominent position in government with perhaps a specific department with relevant expertise on a permanent basis:

> I think [there could be] some kind of cultural committee, no not committee, bad word, group that are able to take a strategy for Hong Kong as a whole, in terms of cultural development and cultural

protection – and heritage conservation that has some authority and power to deal with things.

(I5)

There has been talk of setting up a new entity within government called the Culture Bureau to fulfil this role but whether this will be carried through is yet unclear.

Creating incentives

Given that the government is going down the route of allowing NGOs to run sites, it was felt important that a good policy context and proper incentives for good management (including interpretation and interpretive programmes) be set:

> Good policies need to be constantly reviewed and updated. So, I'd lay the blame on management. I go back to the fact that good site management includes the management of its interpretation. And I think that should be a part of any obligation on the part of an operator.
>
> (I2)

In being more "hands-off", the government has to lay down more specific requirements for storytelling, public education programming and interpretation for the eventual operators of sites. This requires them to understand what they want in terms of interpretive outcomes, to be able to project forward in terms of the specifics of the site, couch this in sufficiently binding but flexible contractual terms and be able to judge operational management plans and whether there is sufficient and effective interpretive provision included in them:

> The project level is easier. It's easier as I'd say, for example, in the revitalisation scheme, kind of administered by the government. There are requirements for public access for a guided tour. But there are no requirements on the details of the tour. That could be developed. I don't see any reason why that when we develop a set of conservation guidelines on the hardware side, why couldn't we ask for something for the historic side?
>
> (I1)

Having provided the scaffolding for incorporating interpretation into the project structure contractually, it was felt that the government could do more to incentivise doing interpretation well or at all. Part of the difficulty in this is how to specify, measure and quantify the interpretive outcomes of such projects:

> There are requirements, usually in the brief, to have some form of interpretation. And it's how you deal with that, how you interpret the need for interpretation. If you put some graphic panels in the corner room of a space, are you ticking the box or not? Is it about messaging? Is it about your archive or how you've preserved artefacts within the site or about how you preserve the building space, how you reuse the space. The question is really, how do you quantify that?
>
> (I5)

However, there are the international and regional awards for conservation which include requirements for interpretation such as the UNESCO Asia-Pacific Award for Cultural Heritage Conservation but it was felt that perhaps the Hong Kong government could find a way to recognise interpretive activity within a project specifically, given that it is seen as a weak element in many of the heritage revitalisation projects:

> I would say, "Have you thought about an incentive program? Rewarding sites that do a good job of interpretation?" You know, why not? Because it's very clear it's necessary to move things along. We reward people for doing good conservation work, you know, knowing how to do the right mortar mix, so why shouldn't we be rewarding people for doing good interpretation?
>
> (I2)

Establishing an independent body to oversee issues of historical narrative

There were some strong opposing views amongst participants about whether it was necessary to set up an authority to oversee the way Hong Kong's story is told across the range of heritage projects with a public communication remit.

On the one hand the lack of any authority to create some sort of consistency across storytelling heritage properties in Hong Kong seemed like a retreat from responsibility:

> Where is the guardian? Where, ultimately, is the territory-wide level body that is tasked with taking care of these matters? Of recording, logging, of initiating and executing and policing these activities? And I just don't see it.
>
> (I3)

There are a number of successful examples of public communication of heritage through the activities of heritage trusts. The National Trust of Australia (New South Wales), with its intention to become "a genuine gateway for the entire heritage community" provides a varied communication programme including the quarterly publication of the National Trust Magazine, its website and the new Heritage Space community forum. The UK's National Trust is unique in its evolution but nevertheless has useful lessons in terms of the prioritisation of visitor access, and a very effective public information and media strategy and presence. Its messaging strategy about the value of the nation's heritage and the story it has to tell is a key strength in building credibility and support from its membership and the wider public. Alongside this, the strong educational and research capabilities of English Heritage, as well as its ability to operate properties, is worthy of consideration for emulation.

Heritage trusts around the world are not without their critics. Some of them, like the National Trust or English Heritage, wield enormous (some say disproportionate) cultural power and influence. Owning some of the world's most ancient and iconic man-made structures, such as the UK's Stonehenge, they have become a focus both for positive action and negative reaction. Some of this scepticism derives from the perception that these organisations are effectively vehicles to channel public money into conserving the heritage of a privileged class of landed aristocracy. Could a Hong Kong Heritage Trust conceivably been seen to be at the beck and call of a small, wealthy elite bent only on the preservation of their dynastic mansions? Possibly, but it should be noted that designation from a heritage trust also usually comes with responsibilities of providing public access that might otherwise not exist. It might also provide a conduit for private individuals who may wish to leave their historic properties to the state but who might not be willing to turn it over to a government department better known for its land development. So, it seems that looking at overseas examples suggested the need for some sort of authority, possibly independent, to have some form of credibility and effectiveness to raise the profile of cogently interpreting a narrative across a number of sites without being subject to vacillating political considerations:

> The National Trust and the whole kind of planning regime in, for example, the U.K. seems to be much more cogent and maybe even too powerful. But it has teeth and can force things to happen. We don't seem to have that here.... Perhaps we should be setting up an independent body, an independent authority to deal with these things. An authority which has the power to make these controversial decisions without reference to government.... Take it out of government, give it

independence as a statutory body, populate it with expertise and allow it to have budget allocation power for projects on a prioritized basis or whatever. And allow it to then direct – properly direct – consultants in what is required to be done.

(I3)

The creation of some form of independent or charitable trust was seen as key to circumventing the government's nervousness about being responsible for tackling the contested nature of Hong Kong's story, so releasing a potential bottle-neck to the progress of projects:

> I think establishing a charitable trust of some sort, building preservation trust or whatever you want to call it would be a way of reconciling that issue because, once set up, it will then be self-governing and it doesn't need to be anything to do with government. And that will be a way of government enabling this initiative to develop, but without acquiring undue amounts of criticism from what might go wrong or accrue criticism in the future.

(I4)

It was felt that it would be important for this body to be multi-disciplinary in order to avoid the silo mentality of government departments previously identified:

> I think an overarching body that dealt with anything on a citywide level would be a starting point. Having a cultural heritage department that is focused not just on reuse but also on fostering culture and developing it. That I think needs consideration as well. That then in turn might lead to more relevant reuse of buildings and sites.... A body that would oversee, I don't know, the connection between the intangible heritage and the physical entities of heritage within the city would be useful.

(I5)

However, there was disagreement whether this body should have a thorough auditing role of the Hong Kong narrative to try to create a focal point for consistency and continuity across projects. This would not only provide a functional role of implementing consistency across interpretive experiences in Hong Kong but also provide a symbolic elevation of the role of interpretation in projects by establishing a necessary hurdle by which projects are judged by an outside entity; just as projects need to meet such practical benchmarks as engineering or fire standards. However, there was the concern expressed that an auditing function would be too prescriptive and possibly would get bogged down in controversy:

> I'm not sure whether we need any auditing organization and certainly not authority to define what actually happened in a particular time, in a particular place. But I think I would like to see that the government could work hard to provide and facilitate the amalgamation of information and sharing of information through the society as a whole, without actually kind of defining what is right or wrong.
>
> (I1)

Again, the government-oriented view seems to prefer a more ad hoc arrangement whereby individual non-government organisations through trial and error present a range of perspectives on Hong Kong's story, overseen by the appropriate government departments.

Hong Kong society is changing

Even with changes to the way government does things and the administrative structure of cultural and heritage projects, there is a sense that the situation will probably get worse before it gets better:

> I'm not particularly optimistic. Even if we do have a Culture Bureau in the future, it will still be relatively low on the government agenda. While I'm saying that, I'm still struggling on a daily basis to try to appeal to the general public, the Hong Kong citizen. Hong Kong's history, appreciation of history in Hong Kong is very important before you can appreciate buildings and places.
>
> (I1)

However, there is also the feeling that things are changing and a growing sense of identity in Hong Kong will contribute to increased awareness of the importance of heritage and its role in shaping the way people see themselves:

> When people start to wake up and smell the coffee, so to speak, when they realize that "Actually I *do* have a voice" and "This *is* mine. This is my home, this is where I live, this is who I am and I am of *this* place. Therefore, I need to engage with it in some way. I need to express my opinion about it." And that seems to be happening more and more. The limitation on that is whether or not the government is able to catch up quickly enough; to be nimble enough to deal with this.
>
> (I3)

This primarily seems to be a generational phenomenon with an older generation in senior positions of government lagging behind a younger generation which identifies more strongly with a purely Hong Kong identity:

> What we kept seeing, particularly the pre-1980s period, is how people describe Hong Kong as a "borrowed place, borrowed time". A lot of people who were actually here for decades believed that one day we'll go back to Mainland China. That's the homeland. There's only those baby-boomers who kind of subconsciously developed a kind of attachment. That's my generation.
>
> (I1)

And as more revitalisation projects come on stream and are completed, it is expected that experience of these types of project will build in Hong Kong:

> The revitalisation scheme of particular projects like CPS (Central Police Station) will provide enough critical mass to make a difference in all sorts of ways. The trade skills being one, the understanding on the part of other professionals, government officials and so on, hopefully will be affected by projects like CPS.
>
> (I4)

Figure 3.1 The Tai Kwun Centre for Heritage and Arts: situated in the former Central Police Station compound is one of the most significant revitalisation projects in Hong Kong and possibly the region.

Source: Neil Williams.

Table 3.1 Summary of key points derived from the interviews

What are good and less good examples of heritage revitalisation in Hong Kong and why?

Category	Example	Why?
Good	Tai O Police Station	Successful by Hong Kong standards
		Recognised by UNESCO award
		Links with the community
	PMQ	Reasonably successful adaptive re-use
Less good	1881 Heritage	Over-commercialised
		Exclusive, high-end brands
		Poor conservation
		Destruction of unique aspects of the site
		Lack of meaningful interpretation
	Aberdeen/Ap Lei Chau Waterfront	Lack of narrative
		Lack of interpretation
		Lack of content
	Wedding Card Street	Demolition of original fabric
		Creation of fake heritage
		Loss of both tangible and intangible heritage
	PMQ	Lack of interpretation to understand the original use of the site
	Murray House	Lack of storytelling and interpretation

Why does the story get lost in the end result of such projects when the original stated purpose was to tell the story of the site?

Summary	Elaboration
Political expediency	It's about the Hong Kong Government having to retain a site and adaptively re-use. The need to tell its story is an add-on.

Lack of experience in government	Civil servants trying to interfere with complex and sensitive projects despite lack of experience.
Lack of interest and engagement with subject matter	An assumed lack of public interest in history and heritage, translates into over-emphasis on hardware of conservation, i.e. privileging the building over the story.
Risk aversion to a contested history	De-emphasis of history education during the Colonial period followed by a tendency to avoid controversial or contested history post-Handover in a risk-averse civil service.
Early stage of heritage attraction development	Hong Kong is at an early stage of developing what might be termed a heritage industry and so is still developing the appropriate skills and talent.

How does the way that revitalisation projects are structured affect the quality of the interpretation?

Hard to quantify interpretation	Tenders are intended to define parameters and setting open-ended briefs makes tenderers nervous.
Commercialised, cost-conscious context	These projects are complex and costly. Interpretation may only be considered at the point of the project when finances have become constrained.
Consultants want government to provide more coherent briefs	Those who set the tenders need to put more thought into how they see the content being communicated.
The government side wants to set more open briefs	Those who set the tenders prefer to give greater scope for NGOs etc to interpret the content. This is seen by consultants as a flight from responsibility.
Government does not see telling Hong Kong's story as its responsibility	Those who set the tenders prefer to see those outside government set the boundaries of interpretation and storytelling through a free market mechanism.

continued

Table 3.1 Continued

What steps should the Hong Kong Government take to promote interpretation within heritage revitalisation projects?

Summary	Elaboration
Capacity building	The private sector sees the need to enable the senior level of civil service management to be confident and capable of dealing and engaging with interpretation and narrative. The public sector view was more along the lines of building capacity such as maintaining data sources to enable agencies or individuals outside of government to engage in interpretive activities.
Creating the right market environment	Hong Kong's free market economy was seen to be a successful model to bring new expertise into heritage revitalisation within a context set by government.
Resolving where the responsibility should lie in government	The role of overseeing heritage-related projects should be given a more prominent position in government with perhaps a specific department with relevant expertise on a permanent basis. Could this be the possible establishment of a Culture Bureau?
Creating incentives	More specific requirements of interpretive outcomes needed for operators with an aspiration to create projects worthy of awards such as UNESCO.
Establishing an independent body	This would be an independent, multidisciplinary authority to provide a focus for revitalisation and interpretive activity with credibility to oversee issues of historical narrative for Hong Kong.

How will social changes in Hong Kong affect interpretation in these projects going forward?

A growing sense of a permanent Hong Kong identity	This will contribute to increased awareness of the importance of heritage and its role in shaping the way people see themselves, especially with a younger generation redefining Hong Kong's story.

Summary of findings

Table 3.1 summarises the key points derived from the interviews. The questions as summarised represent the general direction of the conversations as they developed in an iterative, flexible fashion rather than strictly adhering to a set list of questions.

4 Implications for interpretation in heritage revitalisation

Hong Kong tourism has for decades relied on the "East meets West" narrative, but will this be sufficient to satisfy an increasingly sophisticated global and local cultural tourism audience? The need to define a series of independent or interlocking narratives which communicate a story about Hong Kong that resonates with an increasingly activist public across a growing portfolio of heritage tourism attractions potentially puts the role of interpretation at the forefront of tourism product development for Hong Kong.

The Hong Kong Tourism Board intends to focus on cultural tourism to try to tap into a growing international market, highlighting arts and culture as the core experiences on offer in Hong Kong. This means greater and accelerated development of cultural and heritage attractions, including heritage revitalisation projects. The redevelopment of the Avenue of Stars and the Tsim Sha Tsui promenade is due to be complete by 2020 and, in the same year, it is expected that major venues in the West Kowloon Cultural District, including visual culture museum M+, the Xiqu Centre, Freespace, the Lyric Theatre Complex and the park will be finished. The HK$4.1 billion East Kowloon Cultural Centre will be delivered by 2021. Historical buildings such as the Yau Ma Tei Theatre, which showcases young Cantonese opera talent, and the Jao Tsung-I Academy, formerly the Lai Chi Kok Hospital, will also be refurbished. All of these new cultural facilities and revitalised heritage sites such as PMQ and the Central Police Station Compound, renamed the Tai Kwun Centre for Heritage and Art in 2018, have become a major focus for the Tourism Commission to position Hong Kong not simply as a place to eat, drink and shop. The role of interpretation, the project process in which it operates and the interaction between the public sector commissioning heritage revitalisation projects and the private/NGO sector which implements them is key in creating meaningful experiences for tourists. What conclusions, then, can we draw for the future from our investigations into the current state of interpretive planning in heritage revitalisation projects in Hong Kong?

Reflection on the original assumptions

In the conceptual design of this study (Figure 2.3) certain assumptions were made about what seemed to be a diminution of the role of interpretation in heritage revitalisation projects and the reasons for it, namely: the constraints of the Hong Kong government as client, the misunderstanding of the interpretive planning field itself, the nature of the heritage revitalisation field in Hong Kong and commercial pressures on the eventual product. How many of these were borne out by the findings of the qualitative research analysis?

The original assumptions were generally reflected (in some cases exactly) by the research analysis (see Figure 4.1) and concrete steps to remedy some of the perceived issues emerged (see Figure 4.2). In terms of the constraints of the Hong Kong government as a client, the lack of experience of commissioning such projects within the civil service was corroborated with the research findings. However, the assumption about the loss of institutional memory in government hampering the retention of expertise seemed less important than a simple unwillingness to engage with the "difficult" subject of Hong Kong's history. Moreover, the idea of an inflexible civil service system being a contributory constraint was reinforced by the finding of political expediency meaning that processes were carried out for their own sake rather than for the good of projects. Added to this was a risk-averse culture within government which was borne out by the interviews. So, aspects of the original assumptions are validated by the research and further evidence and examples of constraints were highlighted, such as a lack of interest and engagement with the subject matter. Possibly this was due to the sense of trepidation at being held responsible, as well as the government not seeing telling Hong Kong's story as its role. The dichotomy arose of consultants wanting the government to provide more coherent briefs whilst the government side seems to want to set more open briefs.

Within the interpretive planning field, the original assumptions that the role of interpretation was ill-defined without well-recognised standards and that it was a niche service not well understood within certain sections of the heritage attraction design industry were reflected by the acknowledgement by the interviewees that Hong Kong is at an early stage of heritage attraction development. This need for specialist involvement for such public works projects and the requirement for government to adapt their processes to it was both a key assumption and result of the research. The context of the Hong Kong government's recent conversion to the cause of conservation and the resulting flurry of activity in the heritage revitalisation field was seen as significant to assessing the current role of interpretation in such projects. The assumption that clearly identifiable commercial benefits, with a requirement for a greater degree of self-funding and with the income from retail, food and beverage easy to quantify, was a contributory factor to the relegation of interpretive planning within projects was also correlated. There was a general feeling that, with such a public demand for adaptive re-use of buildings with appropriate content, the field will move forward quickly and the government will be forced to keep up.

Returning to our hypotheses of Figure 2.5 depicting the perceived reduction of representation of interpretation in the finished heritage revitalisation project compared to the initial perceived importance, anecdotal findings suggest that the rate of decline of the profile of interpretation within the project is not linear as originally surmised but proceeds in graduated steps.

This happens as the tender for design or design and build approaches, and then post-tender as commercial concerns become more pressing, to finally level out at a much lower level than initially intended. It seems mainly due to the governmental imperative to be seen to be telling the story which ensures that the mission to tell the story of the site is contained in the tender (even if in a somewhat more watered-down version than at

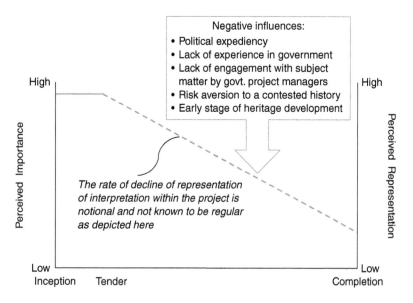

Figure 4.1 Factors bearing down on the interpretive element of a heritage revitalisation project.

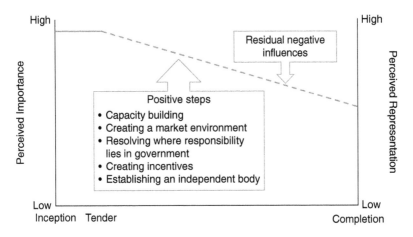

Figure 4.2 Potential factors to maintain the interpretive element through the course of a heritage revitalisation project.

inception), followed by a lack of mechanisms to maintain its role in the project as commercial pressures come to bear in the latter implementation and operational preparation stages for opening. We summarise the findings of possible steps that could be taken to counter these negative influences in Figure 4.2.

The applications of results

The development of a methodology to create heritage revitalisation projects and the role of interpretive planning within it has been an iterative process over the past 30 or so years and will no doubt continue to be so. However, by being more aware and analytical of shortcomings and possibilities within the development of process, there may be opportunities to speed up the progress of integrating interpretation more fully into such heritage tourism products, thereby minimising any further sub-standard outcomes, saving both time and public money. This exploratory study aims to contribute to that growing awareness and more analytical approach. So, how might this research and its conclusions be applied?

Hong Kong finds itself at the confluence of a number of unique currents of post-colonial economic, political and social development and with this is coming a greater realisation of a need for more meaningful cultural and heritage tourism products for both a local and international audience. However, whilst every place's history is unique, there are some factors about the level of development of conservation and heritage revitalisation (early), the historical sensitivities (post-colonial) and nature of public sector governance (hidebound but seeking more opportunities for cooperation with the private sector) that make the findings of this study more widely applicable in markets with one or more of these conditions. They suggest that improvements to the integration of the role of interpretation in the development of heritage tourism products in Hong Kong need to be holistic, and across public, private and non-governmental sectors. The study has identified a number of positive steps (Figure 4.2) that can be taken to raise the profile and efficacy of interpretive planning within such projects. These positive steps require action from both public and private sectors of the heritage revitalisation sphere to bolster the role of storytelling throughout the life cycle of the project development to ensure that it is represented in some significant way in the product outcome.

A new theoretical model

If we refer back to our adapted model of Timothy and Boyd's heritage tourism experience (Figure 2.4) we can map these findings and steps as direct actions and outcomes in order to positively affect the heritage tourism experience going forward.

The process of heritage experience development has been divided into public and private hemispheres. A key finding of the research is the need to ensure that the public and private sectors are doing what they are respectively most suited to. The previous categories of "authenticity", "impact management" and "conservation" remain unchanged but fall into the public sector for the two former (with government departments being the arbiter and certifier through grading schemes of site authenticity, as well as usually the guardians of the site condition) and "conservation" the latter (with outside expertise usually needing to be brought in by governments departments). Improved governance will require capacity building to improve the civil service's understanding and administration of these complex projects, as well as resolving where responsibility lies within government for management and policy. This will enable the creation of the right market environment for the most beneficial interaction between private expertise and public governance. Part of setting the right market conditions for success will be creating the right incentives for companies to deliver on high standards of conservation and interpretation, all of which will have a beneficial effect on the outcome of the eventual heritage tourism experience. Both the actions of the established procedures within the public sphere and the evolving process of the private sector in relation to their roles in heritage revitalisation projects

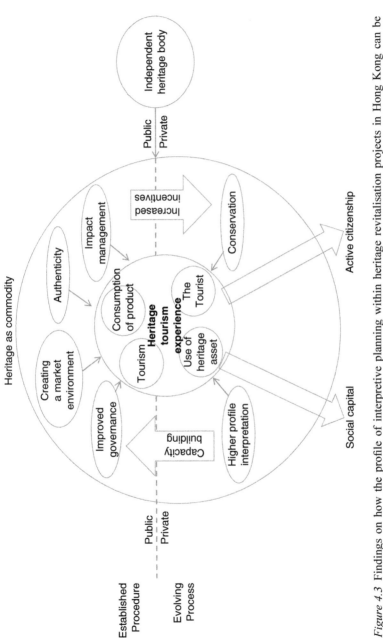

Figure 4.3 Findings on how the profile of interpretive planning within heritage revitalisation projects in Hong Kong can be raised mapped onto an adapted Timothy and Boyd's model of heritage tourism experience with McKercher and Du Cros' tourism framework.

could be overseen by an independent heritage body, holding to account both public and private players.

The government would appear to still have the most pivotal role in setting the conditions for the success of heritage revitalisation projects in Hong Kong. The new theoretical model could be used by government as a potential checklist of ways by which it can enhance its commissioning and overseeing of these heritage and cultural tourism initiatives. It has a key role in looking across the sphere of heritage revitalisation as represented by the model as a whole and setting the optimum pre-conditions for the successful interaction and cooperation between the public, private and any potential independent heritage trust. However, this does require a degree of openness and to some extent bravery on behalf of the government to be willing to genuinely engage with the community and potentially controversial aspects of Hong Kong's story.

The creative industries might use the theoretical model to help ensure that interpretive planning and development is given sufficient time and resources within the project to meet the needs of the attraction development process and, it is hoped, so improve the end outcome. In light of this, the role of interpretation within the project and the context of the heritage revitalisation sphere as a whole could be highlighted to the client specifically as a concern and the appropriate skilled personnel either within the client and/or creative team be given the status within the project they deserve.

The increasingly aware body of activists, civic groups and interested members of the general public might use the findings and model to hold the government accountable for giving interpretation sufficient weight within the overall revitalisation process to ensure that the collective memory of the local community and those with an emotional stake in a site are included in the development and articulation of the site's story and the ongoing management of its narrative. This might be done through regular consultations or, preferably, through interactive workshops.

From the academic point of view, the theoretical model may raise a series of issues that could be further explored or elaborated upon with further research studies.

Beyond Hong Kong, emerging heritage tourism attractions, cities or states might be able to derive some instructive ideas about how to structure governance and tendering, interactions between the relevant public and private spheres, their products or heritage attraction delivery processes. This is particularly true of tourism markets at a relatively early stage of developing or adaptively re-using their built heritage for tourism purposes that wish to create mixed use attractions that require the collaboration of public and private sectors. Around the world, there is no shortage of potential heritage attractions that have contested histories which require well-structured public/ private project and policy coordination to tell their stories.

Limitations on the inclusion of contemporaneous developments

During the course of conducting the research for this study a series of developments took place in the sphere of heritage conservation in Hong Kong that may have an impact on the role of interpretation in heritage revitalisation projects going forward. In particular, there has been a growing demand for a recognition of a distinctly Hong Kong identity.

A commentary in the *South China Morning Post* (Cheung, 20 October 2015) characterised Hong Kong as an 18-year old with an identity crisis. Caught between a sense that Hong Kong's success as a capitalist city lies in the economic, legal, social, governmental, educational and cultural foundations laid during the British era – its colonial heritage – and demands to become ever more integrated with Mainland China, the people of Hong Kong seem to be going through a struggle for the right to define their own city's image on the world stage.

The public opposition to the national security legislation of the Basic Law Article 23 in 2003, the introduction of national education in 2012 and the rise of a wide range of activist groups such as Scholarism and Hong Kong Indigenous has seen the growth of a form of Hong Kong "localism" which promotes perceived local interests first and foremost. The 79-day Occupy Central phenomenon that drew up to 100,000 demonstrators in 2014 and resulted in around 1,000 arrests was a pro-democracy movement that deeply divided Hong Kong society across broadly generational lines. Not only did it bring together a wide range of opposition activists, but it also resulted in an outpouring of artistic and cultural expression that, along with the unprecedented numbers, demonstrated the depth of feeling among certain sectors of the city about the need to define Hong Kong in contrast to the Mainland.

The outcry over the demolition of the Star Ferry Pier in 2006 and the active efforts made to preserve Queen's Pier showed a growing recognition, especially among younger people, that certain places have a value to society which goes beyond the physical structures associated with them. The Star Ferry Pier, built in the 1950s, was neither old nor very impressive architecturally. Over time, the practicality and pleasure which people have associated with the ferry itself became embodied in the place engendering an emotional value and collective memory. The so-called "Fishball" riots at Chinese New Year 2016 where radical localist groups violently confronted the police over the traditional selling of hawker food on the streets of Mongkok shows that, at least amongst a section of the student population, there is no need for any further convincing regarding the importance of protecting intangible culture; some young Hongkongers are willing to put their bodies on the line and even go to jail for it. Bland (2017) calls these young people "Generation HK" and states that

> for many members of Generation HK, the growing tensions between China and Hong Kong have crystallised the feeling that their home has its own unique character that needs to be protected.... With the clock ticking down to 2047, the struggle to define what it means to be a Hong Konger will intensify.

More peaceably, civil society organisations are emerging to lobby on various issues and NGOs are starting to be formed to operate particular sites. As these organisations develop, scope is likely to exist for this third economic sector to play a significantly greater role in heritage conservation and management. These are positive signs, demonstrating that the public judges heritage conservation to be a phenomenon for the common good over which they should have some direct ownership and with which they should engage. A study of the way that myths used by tourism to promote Hong Kong as a unique destination has shown that they lean heavily on the distinctiveness of a kind of postcolonial hybridity. Zhang *et al.* (2015) highlight the importance of interpretation within an increasing number of heritage tourism projects in the process of defining this new identity and the potential for dissonance in the complex landscape of Hong Kong identity politics if this process is ignored.

Internal/external validity issues

The privileged position of being an industry insider with access to key players in the heritage revitalisation field in Hong Kong also brings with it a certain amount of professional baggage in terms of assumptions and relationships with existing or potential clients or creative collaborators. By its very nature this subjectivity is hard to assess dispassionately but its potential influence must be recognised. It should also be recognised that the necessarily small sample of interviewees was dominated by white, middle-class, Western-educated men. This is the by-product of the small professional and cultural pool from which consultants (albeit those with decades of experience within the Hong Kong cultural, heritage and creative sector) have been drawn by both the Hong Kong government and this study. However, as we have seen, things are changing rapidly in this field and it is expected that, should a similar study be conducted in the near future, there will be more ethnically Hong Kong Chinese professionals available with relevant experience to draw from.

Future research opportunities

As an exploratory study in an under-researched field, this study delineates the broad theoretical landscape of issues related to the role of interpretation in heritage revitalisation projects in Hong Kong. Further studies may benefit from drilling down into specific projects to examine the processes and interactions between participants as a case study or perhaps widening its scope to include other post-colonial societies. In particular, it may be a fruitful line of research to try to pinpoint more accurately at what key points in the project process, notionally outlined in Figure 2.5, that the status of storytelling within the overall product begins to be substantially diminished. This may throw up particular practical steps that might be taken to improve institutional and knowledge management of participants through the analysis of specific practices, tender procedures or project management. As the pool of home grown practitioners grows, it will be of value to conduct a similar study in a few years' time to see how the situation and perceptions of it have changed. Allied or separate to this could be an examination of the outcomes of such projects through measuring visitor satisfaction of the delivery of interpretation of on-site storytelling and educational programming, as well as the impact of any future new developments such as civic pressures groups or NGOs.

Despite its late start in the heritage conservation field, Hong Kong has the potential to find itself in the forefront of interpretation of heritage revitalisation projects regionally. This will require monitoring and evaluation of current ongoing and future projects, academically and professionally rigorous analysis and benchmarking of processes and outcomes, and the application of international standards and theories of urban heritage. The public currently seem to be ahead of the government on the value they place on both the tangible and intangible culture of Hong Kong's urban fabric; to maintain progress in this field it is hoped that both the government and creative industries engage with and further explore the issues raised in this study.

References

Bland, B. (2017). *Generation HK*. Australia: Penguin Random House.
Cheung, S. (20 October 2015). "An orphan, an angst-ridden teenager or a cross-cultural traveler? Hong Kong must find its unique identity". *South China Morning Post*, Insight & Opinion.

Index

Page numbers in **bold** denote tables, those in *italics* denote figures.

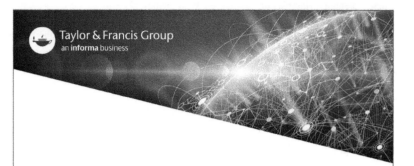